Golden Words of Yore

Puranamityeva na sadhu sarvam
na capi kavyam navamityavadyam
Santah parikṣyanyatarad bhajante
mudhah parapratyayaneyabuddhih

A book is not sacred simply because it is ancient; nor is a book to be ignored simply because it is recently written. The wise give recognition to a work on its merit; fools echo others' opinions.

The Malavikagmimitram

AF795997

Insights In Nadis (Discover your Dharma)

Compiled by
Andrée Leclerc

Cover Design By
Saptarishis Astrology

© **Saptarishis Publications** 2014
1st Edition 2014
1st Reprint 2017, 2nd Reprint 2021

Proofing & Editing by :
Andrée Leclerc

Published and Distributed by :
Saptarishis Astrology
Plot No.5, Sunlight Residency
Defence Enclave, Sector-44, Som Bazar Road,
Near Steller Green Apartment, Noida - 201303, U.P.
Tel: +91 981 995 7779
Email: admin@saptarishisastrology.com

Designed by:
Mrinal Kanti Kesh & Kanchan Chatterjee

For sale in India: ₹ 351/- For sale outside India: $ 20/-

© Copyright Violation
No part of this book may be reproduced in any form or by any means including but not exclusively the right of translation in other languages without prior written permission of the publisher except in the case of brief quotations, in any language, embodied in critical articles and/or reviews. Without written permission of the publisher one cannot make any youtube video on any technique posted in this book. It would lead to copyright infringement & legal case.

ISBN: 978-8-192-96790-5

Insights In Nadis

INSIGHTS IN NADIS

DISCOVER YOUR DHARMA

As told by

Sri Late A. V. Sundaram

And compiled by

Andrée Leclerc

SAPTARISHIS PUBLICATIONS

Complier's Note

Dear Readers,

This is not a regularly authored book on astrology and similar subjects. Rather, the Nadis presented here were narrated by Sri A.V. Sundaram-ji from what he has heard, read, researched and learned from various sources and various times. This collection of Nadis is part of the astrological gems he gathered in the course of his 35 years in the astrological journey.

The readers (you!) are cautioned to go slowly in accepting and applying these principles. This compilation is retold without chapters and divided in sessions with no continuity.

We are very thankful to Saptarishi Astrology for bringing this collection to the Lovers of Nadi Jyotish. Kudos!

May you all be super Lucky!

Andrée Leclerc

P.S. You will find herein dicta floating about on some pages – these have been collected from Nadi works by Mr. Sundaram-ji.

The cover image shows the Navagrahas as seen in a mirror.

Contents

Session 1 - Basics

Introduction – Nadis as Applied to Jyotish

Since India covers much ground as the 7th largest country on the planet, with 28 states, 7 unions and 22 official languages, the same knowledge may adopt varied names in different regions. Therefore, our subject of study is known as Nadi in the south and as Samhita in the northern area. Nadis are written on palm leaves and are known as OLE in Sri Lanka. Samhitas are hand written.

NADIS are classified in two parts:
JIVA NADI and AJIVA NADI

- Jiva Nadis are known as the speaking Nadis which are generally used in Nadi readings.
- Ajiva Nadis are known as Abyhasa Nadis (practicing). These are divided into Mantra Nadi and Tantra Nadi.

It is said that there are 72 Nadis in existence: 36 representing Mantra Nadis and 36 Tantra Nadis in addition to some Prashna Nadis. It is also said that Mantra Nadis and Tantra Nadis each comprise over one lakh (100,000) charts.

Nadi astrological dicta or remedial measures are all taken from AJIVA to be used in regular astrological practice

History according to Nadis

#1 First, there was the UNIVERSE and that is the HOROSCOPE.

#2 Then came TIME and SPACE and these were shown by the SUN and MOON. From these we obtained the TITHI which is DISTANCE.

#3 To populate #1 and #2, the INDIVIDUAL, EARTH and the REST OF SPACE was created and these are represented by, respectively, the LAGNA, RAHU and KETU.

#4 To place these in perspective, the notions of DHARMA, ARTHA, KAMA and MOKSHA were brought forth to join with the Rashis of FIRE, EARTH, AIR and WATER.

#5 To define and personify further the PANCHA BHUTAS or 5 ELEMENTS, the Grahas SATURN, JUPITER, MARS, MERCURY and VENUS were each granted a specific element, namely and respectively AIR, ETHER, FIRE, EARTH and WATER (now this may seem confusing as we already mentioned Rahu for Earth above but to clarify, Rahu would be "The Planet Earth" and all that goes on over there like what you see and don't see on TV, whereas Mercury is the element "Earth" that is, the "solid stuff" in things – i.e. the parts of the TV itself).

#6 For the 6 GUNAS: KAMA, LOBHA, KRODHA, MOHA, MADA and MATSARYA which are reflected by the SATVARGAS.

#7 Is the COMPLETION or "THE END". Seven senses, seven colours of the rainbow, seven organs. Completion of anything is represented by the number 7. Per example, the Janma Lagna is completed by the 7H i.e. death – or, the 6H for working and the 12H for rest. 7 Rishis, 7 mountains, 7 seas...

#8 TERMINATES. Meaning that at this point, things are no longer in our Hands – or we could say that what goes on there is beyond the mind.

#9 REPEATS the past i.e. rebirth.

JUPITER'S SPECIAL STATUS

In Nadi Jyotish, JUPITER is known as JIVA and its Moolatrikona sign, SAGITTA- RIUS, is used as JIVA's standard starting point. Consequently, you will note that we will refer to the chart with Sagittarius as LAGNA in some instances. Nevertheless, since the sign of ARIES is the classical first sign of KALAPURUSHA, we will also venture obser- vations and presentation of data from this sign as well. To brief you on the reason why this is so, Nadi considers that all charts should be read from Kalapurusha-Aries since this indicates what FATE we were born with. The Lagna (any Lagna) is where our past life joins this one and shows what we should be expected to accomplish in this life.

The term "LAGNA" means "TO JOIN".
The term "ASCENDANT" means
"THAT WHICH RISES ON THE EAST"

Therefore, the first implies the two elements of PAST and FUTURE coming toge- ther whereas the second is taken from an astronomical fact.

GRAHAS KARAKATWAS

SUN	King, famous, father, son, Sunday, Atma Karaka
MOON	Hindu and rivers (Ganga etc.), food, Monday, mother or mother-in-law for married lady, elderly woman, eldest sister, daily cash, debts, the act of cheating
MARS	Land, siblings, husband, Tuesday
MERCURY	Small, budhi, birds, parrots, colours, Wednesday, friend, does not cheat like the Moon if Moon is not involved – more self- centered than cheater
JUPITER	Gurus, temples, peaceful, soft, wealth, Thursday, Jiva karaka i.e. self, 16 kinds of wealth, living tree i.e. has water, when Jup transits over natal Moon it shows a change of residence (same if transiting in trine to Moon: 5 – 9)
VENUS	Beauty, flowers (rose, jasmine...), smells, Love (Prema), poetry, cash $ and dollars wealth, Friday, wife, elder sister or sister-in-law, 2nd eldest, like tamarind it arouses sex
SATURN	Servant, drainage, Saturday, Karma karaka, large intestine until the anus, movement, profession, activity

RAHU	Meaningless, Muslim, unusual, names starting with "R", terrace with no roof, dry wood, seeds, testis, mouth, main entrance: check entrance's direction & see if it agrees with Rahu's position
KETU	Long and thin, hair, tail, Moksha, dry grass, beard, rope, flag, see on the hand where Ketu is placed: there will be a flag; anus

RASHIS (SIGNS) – THEIR KARAKATWAS

ARIES:	Central government, passion, enthusiasm, accidents, struggles, pioneers, stubborn, head
TAURUS:	Stability, permanence of things, wealth, arts, pleasures, patience, productivity, endurance, conservatism, face and neck
GEMINI:	Green grass, joining, siblings, communication, marketing, creativity, versatility, indecision, hypocrisy, arms and lungs
CANCER:	Watery, milk, the symbol is not a crab but the 2 nipples of mother, mother figure, older women, home, emotions, happiness, chest and stomach
LEO:	Administration at government state level, entertainment, sports, ambition, generosity, romance, vanity, arrogance, heart
VIRGO:	Business, education, playgrounds, personifies virgin, plain stuff, coins, purity, method, health and disease, setbacks, intestines
LIBRA:	Where business happens i.e. the market place, private parts, kidneys, does not retain urine – good for gathering folks together, popular – is like a market i.e. stuff comes from elsewhere to that place. It is the function of sex as opposed to where babies are manufactured. Harmony, arts, justice
SCORPIO:	Bladder, secretion of urine, cave like, marshy i.e. not liquid & not solid, sinner (with Libra on one side becomes more social) or saint (with Sagittarius on other side becomes wiser). Place

of transition where toxic waste is removed – uterus. Destruction and regeneration, passions, mysteries...

SAGITTARIUS: Forests, religious activities, tradition, legal matters, philosophy, luck, religion, idealism, optimism, fanaticism, indiscipline, hips and thighs

CAPRICORN: Dirty places, mixed nature, perspiration, wet or dry hands – like a soldier who will get dirty in battle but will be clean in training. Will show the two sides while Scorpio hides them. Power, the State, old people and things, responsibility, sobriety, knees

AQUARIUS: Freedom, psychology, inventions, secretive, miser, butcher shop, gambling house, friendship with folks on any level: rich, poor, good, bad... Ankles

PISCES: Reversed, place of pilgrimage, place where we go for a specific purpose and we don't go often Ex: toilet which is given importance only for a time. Infinite, silence, mysticism, escapism, hospitals, jails, feet

Moon conjunct a malefic while that malefic has exchanged place with another planet (parivarthana): the health or character of the mother (Moon) is affected

* * * * * * * * *

Venus alone in own house: wife is from a noble family and of good character

Rashis – Their Attributes

Pisces Meena Moksha - Female Water - Brahmin Dual - Spiritual North	**Aries Mesha** Dharma - Male Fire - Kshatriya Mobile Physical - East	**Taurus Vrishaba** Artha - Female Earth - Vaishya Fixed - Mental South	**Gemini Mithuna** Kama - Male Air - Shudra Dual - Spiritual West
Aquarius Kumbha Kama - Male Air - Shudra Fixed - Mental West	**Rashis and their attributes**		**Cancer Karka** Moksha Female Water - Brahmin Mobile Physical - North
Capricorn Makara Artha - Female Earth - Vaishya Mobile Physical - South	**Leo Simha** Dharma - Male Fire - Kshatriya Fixed - Mental East		
Sagittarius Dhanur Dharma - Male Fire - Kshatriya Dual - Spiritual East	**Scorpio Vrishchika** Moksha Female - Water - Brahmin Fixed - Mental North	**Libra Thula** Kama - Male Air - Shudra Mobile Physical - West	**Virgo Kanya** Artha - Female Earth - Vaishya Dual - Spiritual South

> When transit Saturn comes in the 12th house to natal Venus, one's finances increase

Grahas In Rashis

<table>
<tr>
<td>Pisces
Meena
K Own sign
C Uccha B
Neecha</td>
<td>Aries
Mesha
F Own sign +
Moolatrikona
A Uccha
L Neecha</td>
<td>Taurus
Vrishaba
C Own sign
E Uccha +
Moolatrikona</td>
<td>Gemini
Mithuna
B Own sign</td>
</tr>
<tr>
<td>Aquarius
Kumbha
L Own sign +
Moolatrikona</td>
<td colspan="2" rowspan="2">Own Sign
Moolatrikona
or (Root Sign)
Uccha (Exalted)
Neecha (Fallen)
Leo Simha
A Own sign + Moolatrikona</td>
<td>Cancer
Karka
E Own sign
K Uccha F
Neecha</td>
</tr>
<tr>
<td>Capricorn
Makara
L Own sign
F Uccha K
Neecha</td>
<td></td>
</tr>
<tr>
<td>Sagittarius
Dhanur
K Own sign +
Moolatrikona</td>
<td>Scorpio
Vrishchika
F Own sign
E Neecha</td>
<td>Libra
Thula
C Own sign +
Moolatrikona
L Uccha
A Neecha</td>
<td>Virgo
Kanya
B Own sign +
Moolatrikona
+ Uccha
C Neecha</td>
</tr>
</table>

Check the dispositor of Mars and Venus for after-marriage effects – i.e. Venus for a male chart and Mars for a female chart

NADIS' FRIENDS AND ENEMIES SCHEME

GRAHA	ENEMIES
SUN	Saturn – Rahu – Venus
MOON	Mercury – Venus – Saturn – Rahu
MERCURY	Ketu – Moon – Mars
MARS	Mercury – Saturn – Rahu
VENUS	Sun – Moon – Ketu
JUPITER	Moon
SATURN	Mars – Ketu – Sun – Moon
RAHU	Mars – Moon – Sun
KETU	Mercury – Venus – Saturn

Death takes place when Jupiter transits the mid-point of natal Rahu and Moon

* * * * * * * * *

Jupiter hemmed between Mercury and Mars: dark mark on his back

* * * * * * * * *

Sun, Venus, Mercury conjunction: father has beautiful handwriting or is an artist

BHAVAS (HOUSES)

<table>
<tr>
<td>House 12 •
Losses
Element: Water
Goal: Moksha
Nature: Duhsthana
Classification:
Malefic</td>
<td>House 1 •
The Body
Element: Fire Goal:
Dharma Nature:
Kendra & trine
Classification:
Benefic</td>
<td>House 2 •
Wealth
Element: Earth
Goal: Artha
Nature: Maraka
Classification:
Malefic</td>
<td>House 3 •
Siblings
Element: Air Goal:
Kama Nature:
Uppachaya
Classification:
Neutral</td>
</tr>
<tr>
<td>House 11 •
Earnings
Element: Air Goal:
Kama Nature:
Uppachaya
Classification:
Neutral</td>
<td colspan="2" rowspan="2">Bhavas Elements
Goals Nature
Classification
Significator as
seen from
KALAPURUSHA
House 5 •
Children
Element: Fire Goal: Dharma Nature:
Trine Classification: Benefic</td>
<td>House 4•
Family
relationship
Element: Water
Goal: Moksha
Nature: Kendra
Classification:
Benefic</td>
</tr>
<tr>
<td>House 10 •
Achievement
Element: Earth Goal:
Artha Nature: Kendra
& Uppachaya
Classification:
Benefic</td>
<td></td>
</tr>
<tr>
<td>House 9 •
Knowledge
Element: Fire Goal:
Dharma Nature:
Trine Classification:
Benefic</td>
<td>House 8 •
Life
Element: Water
Goal: Moksha
Nature: Duhsthana
Classification:
Malefic</td>
<td>House 7 •
Spouse
Element: Air Goal:
Kama Nature:
Kendra
& Maraka
Classification:
Neutral</td>
<td>House 6 •
Enemies
Element: Earth
Goal: Artha
Nature: Duhsthana
& Uppachaya
Classification:
Malefic</td>
</tr>
</table>

Karakas For Houses

1H	Sun for one's vigour Moon for one's body
2H	Jupiter for 16 kinds of wealth (children, education, money...) Mercury for speech Venus for family
3H	Mars for brothers and courage Saturn for misery
4H	Venus for conveyances Moon for mother Mercury for learning Mars for property
5H	Jupiter for children Mercury for intelligence
6H	Mars for enemies Saturn for illness
7H	Venus for the wife Mars for passion since he is vigour Mercury for co-wife (i.e. a husband's other wife)
8H	Saturn for longevity and mental suffering

Mars placed in the 10th house from Jupiter: help from brothers

* * * * * * * * * *

Exchange of Venus and Mercury: man has both wife and mistress

* * * * * * * * * *

Mercury and Venus together: pleasure from girlfriend

* * * * * * * * * *

Venus in the 6th house from Mars: delay in marriage and also legal problems in marriage

9H Jupiter for teacher Sun for father and government

10H Sun for power and position
Saturn for service and livelihood
Jupiter for sudden fortune

11H Jupiter for gain and luck of brother

12H Saturn for sorrow Mars for confinement Jupiter for growth and wisdom Ketu for moksha

Check transit Jupiter over natal Ketu for death, marriage, etc. – or Rahu/Ketu's transits over natal Jupiter

* * * * * * * * *

Saturn conjunct Mars: suspicious and cynic

Any planet in conjunction with Rahu or Ketu and exchanging sign with another planet: that planet gets "Naga Dosha". Ex: Saturn + Ketu in Aries and Mars in Capricorn – Mars gets Naga Dosha: death or separation of brothers

MORE ON HOUSES

1- Their Nature

TRINE positions are lucky – things flow on their own: you've got a driver!

KENDRA positions put you to work in order to get where you want to get i.e. you got to drive yourself.

6 – 8 – 12 positions... your car is broken and you've got to push it...

UPPACHAYAS i.e. Houses 3, 6, 10, 11 are all places where the body bends and grows – so growth of the individual is seen through these houses / we need them to go anywhere in life.

Houses	From Jiva's home Sagittarius	Lord
3H: neck	Aquarius	Saturn
6H: hip	Taurus	Venus
10H: knees	Virgo	Mercury
11H: ankles	Libra	Venus

> Sun in the 12th house from Venus: can't save money (if Venus is alone). Check Saturn in the 12th house from Venus for saving money

2- House Lords - Fast Tips

The Janma Lagna (JL) Lord also shows one's very immediate concern i.e. "ME", "YOU and ME" or "US". To find out, see in which sign the Lagna Lord is placed.

THE JANMA LAGNA LORD IS ONE's DESTINY

- If placed in the first 4 signs – ARIES to CANCER – the individual is interested in his/her own interests. Clearly, a "ME" type.
- If placed between LEO and SCORPIO he/she is concerned about the self and the near and dear ones. All about "ME and YOU".
- And if in the 4 last signs – SAGITTARIUS to PISCES – one's considerations include humanity – and they may seek name and fame. "US" for the whole world. As the three Musketeers would say "One for all, all for one!"

> Mercury and Rahu in 2nd house to Sun: one of the children settled in a foreign country

In which sign elements are the Lagna Lord, Sun and Moon placed...?

- FIRE signs indicate one who thinks about the future.
- AIR and EARTH signs give concerns about the present.
- WATER signs retain one's attention in the past.

So, water sign dominated people remember things for a long time (the day I met you, they day you proposed, they day you changed your mind on the proposal thing, the day you married someone else... Alas, what a torture...)

On the whole, discretion comes with the Lagna Lord. It can be influenced if conjunct planets – which can prove frustrating since circumstances or other people's agendas, may always seem to get in the way.

> **Watch it!**
> **An EXALTED planet affects its MOOLATRIKONA rashi!**

See which HOUSE is the Moolatrikona rashi affected. If a planet is exalted, its Moolatrikona can suffer just like a person who is exalted in the outside world can find his/her personal affairs lessened.

THEORY OF KARMA

KARMA is based on the results of actions done during our recurring births. The JANMA LAGNA represents the Present Birth; the 9H represents the PAST BIRTH and the 5H the FUTURE. More about this in the next section "Past, Present and Future".

- What is definitively happening is DRIDHA shown by the DASHAS.
- The results that may or may not happen are ADRIDHA shown by the GOCHARAS.
- Some results may take place and some may not: this is known as DRIDHA/ADRIDHA

The RESULTS of acquired KARMA are GROUPED in THREE WAYS: DRIDHA, ADRIDHA and DRIDHA/ADRIDHA

KARMA which is seen by the YOGAS = some may fructify and some may not fructify.

ONE's KARMA is CATEGORIZED as PRARABDHA, SANCHITA, AGAMI and KRIYAMANA

- PRARABDHA karma is the present day unavoidable reaping of what we sowed in our past life. This is shown by the 6H and 6th Lord

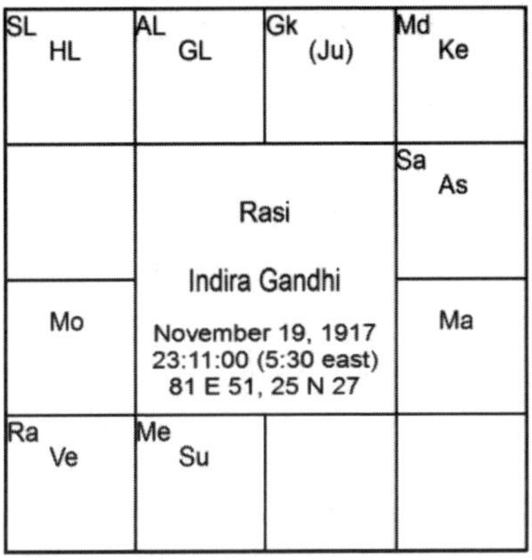

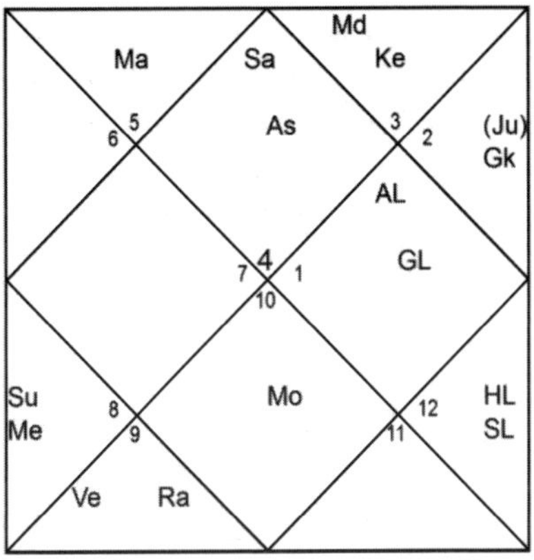

As:	27 Cn 24	Su:	4 Sc 09- DK	Mo:	5 Cp 36- GK	Ma:	16 Le 24- MK
Me:	13 Sc 15- PK	Ju (R):	15 Ta 01- PiK	Ve:	21 Sg 01- AmK	Sa:	21 Cn 48- AK
Ra:	9 Sg 13- BK	Ke:	9 Ge 13	HL:	25 Pi 48	GL:	29 Ar 21

– it is that which we cannot change like being in this life now – or like a coconut tree that can only give coconuts. Here is an example of 6H unalterable karma in the chart of the late Indira Gandhi...

Here, 6th Lord Jupiter occupies the 11H from the Lagna: she had no elder brother but lots of friends. The 11H happens to be the 8H from the 4H of her mother's longevity: she lost her mother early in life. The 11H is the 7H from the 5H: she had two daughters-in-law: one was sent out and the other continued in retaining her power – and so on. 11H is maraka for the 5H: both her children had untimely deaths.

Wherever the 6th Lord representing Prarabdha goes, that bhava can give good or bad results which can't be altered. That's the reason why the 6H stands for sickness and is an uppachaya house of growth – all meant to get the privilege of giving both positive and negative results unexpectedly.

- SANCHITA karma is stored karma that can come anytime so, Sanchita amounts to surprises! This is why a good guy gets troubles and a bad guy gets the goodies – see Houses 1, 5, 9 – these are where Life occurs. Our actions belong to houses 2, 6, 10 with 10H being this present life. 4H is, generally, the place of sto- rage for every life. Now, the storage of our 10H is 4 houses from the 10H...

which takes us to the Lagna! The storage of the 2H of family is the 5H of children and, likewise, the storage of the 6H of Prarabdha is the 9H of ancestors and father. All that deals with houses 1, 5, 9 from any place in the chart can happen suddenly. We can alter the natal 4H which is what we think and fine-tune the 10H of what we do – but not their results.

- AGAMI Karma is what I want to do – my plan – so this is karma in thought process – which is stored in the 4H. If, for whatever reason I don't accomplish something I was really keen on doing in this life by the time I'm gathered to my forefathers, this same desire will be my 12H in my next life. So, 12H comprises all that's pending on my mind.
- KRIYAMANA karma is the actions done in this birth that will determine what we become in the next life – see the 10H... May we judiciously choose our actions...
- In addition, the REGULAR TRANSITS of Rahu/Ketu indicate the inflow and outflow of the karma results.
- 100% KARMA: Rahu/Ketu! Sometimes comes as a kind of "big bang"...
- Any VAKRI planet will finish the left over work from the past life; hence in checking retrogrades, the 9H (past birth Lagna) should be given due consideration.

PAST, PRESENT AND FUTURE – BIRTHS CLASSIFICATION & LIFESPAN

CHANDRA KALA NADI describes NADIAMSAS as follows:

Nadiamsas are 150 parts of a rasi – roughly 12 seconds. Sometimes each Nadi is divided into purva and uttara varga.

- In MOBILE rashis the order of Nadiamsas goes from 1, 2, 3, ... 150 – meaning "starting"
- In FIXED rashis, the order is reversed starting with 150, 149, 148, ... 1 – meaning "the end"

- In DUAL rashis, the sequence starts with 76, 77, 78, ... 150 and then 1 to 75 – meaning "the middle"

Incidentally, the names of all Nadiamsas are female deities' names. Nadiamsas are not equal in division, the smallest being 0 degree 1 minute 4 seconds (0'1'4) to the biggest being 0'3 minutes.

Every individual born in any Lagna will be influenced by its trikona rashis. In all Nadi principles, a division of past, present and future is taken into account. Similarly, this present life could be divided into 3 parts, and the same can be done for the past and future lives – making a total of 9 similar to the Navamsha divisions. The Janma Lagna is the present, the 5H the future birth and the 9H the past birth.

Take the JL of a person. If in a MOBILE sign, the 1st cycle or the 1st third of life is the JL itself. For a DUAL JL, in the 1st cycle the 5H is important, in the 2nd cycle the JL is central and the last third is linked the 9H influences. For FIXED, in the 1st third the 9H is important, then 5H and last the JL – the self – predominates.

In other words, taking the NADIAMSA division: MOBILE rashis show the beginning of life, DUAL show the middle of life and FIXED the end the life

These three parts are determined in time by major life changes. Oftentimes, the first third ends at the age of marriage. So, let's say a person gets married at 28 years, a second important life-changing event occurring at the age of 56 years (28 X 2) would confirm 28 as the key number. Then, by multiplying 28 by 3, we would obtain 84 years as the likely lifespan.

The DIVISION is BASED on the TYPE of RASHI into which the LAGNA is SITUATED

Each of the 3 divisions will be in Houses 1, 5 or 9 and follow this sequence:

MOBILE JL = 1st cycle JL (mobile) – 2nd cycle 9H (dual) – 3rd cycle 5H (fixed)

FIXED JL = 1st cycle 9H (mobile) – 2nd cycle 5H (dual) – 3rd cycle JL (fixed)

DUAL JL = 1st cycle 5H (mobile) – 2nd cycle JL (dual) – 3rd cycle 9H (fixed)

These DIVISIONS also GIVE us HINTS as to the CLIMATE of each THIRD of LIFE

Per example, for persons BORN in a FIXED sign Lagna, they should be advised to keep money for their old age as children may let them down. The self will be more important in the last part of life and this could mean health problems or that one could be in a leadership position – or both... Since the fixed sign Lagna person experiences the 1st cycle in the 9H, these people may have been groomed by their father – such a child should be advised to listen to elders. The 5H as second cycle could bring changes in the career or within one's work, very possibly the birth of children and anything creative or individualistic to the forefront.

Take a lifespan of anywhere from 72 to 80 years in modern time. A major event will take place at the end of the first third of the life – and fix that first 1/3 of life. For example, for a Mobile JL person with Venus in the 9H – if he/she gets married at 28 years, Venus in the 9H becomes the second portion so the second cycle starting in the 9H would be 28 years (further research is needed in this area of fixing lifespan).

We could further expound that for a MOBILE sign starting with the JL cycle, the person as a child may take, on their own accord, some kind of duty in the family or be more interested in learning, performing or any self- development activity. 9H as the second cycle talks of marriage and might be a time for observing traditions and religion or adhering to some form of ethical values. It might also be a period for seeking God and guru. 5H as last cycle could bring a change in career; involve one with children or some kind of counselling, teaching, politics or some creative endeavours.

For a DUAL sign, life starts with the 5H so the child could be lively, curious, creative and independent. Next comes Lagna as second cycle when one may experience the "self" through the activities of a new adult – through work and adjustments of one's self perceptions and out- side life as needed – or possible. With the 9H coming last, the person may be more of a prea- cher for some ideal or do some activity aimed at the public through social work, organizations working for the greater good, politics, etc.

To bring all this to life, let's take the chart of Adolf Hitler born in 1889 – and who lived for 56 years giving an average of 18 years per cycle. (Note: Hitler's biography info was gathered from Wikipedia and varied other web sources.)

So, 1889 + 18 = 1907. This would be the first complete life-change landmark in his pain- filled life.

Then, 1907 + 18 = 1925 for the second life- change landmark.

In fact, 1907 is when his mother died. He was also rejected from the arts academy and, with no financial support from his mother or educational institution, was left on the street. Time kept going and...

He was released from jail in December 1924 and published the first volume of his *Mein Kampf* which described his Nazi political ideology for the first time in 1925. This was the basis for his rise to power a few years later.

MOBILE JL: 1st cycle JL // 2nd cycle 9H // 3rd cycle 5H

Libra is a mobile sign so, the first 18 years' cycle occurs in Libra itself. Saturn the 4th Lord occupies the 4th sign, Cancer, which shows from the start a form of estrangement from the mother and difficulties during childhood. Sat is placed in the 10H which is a maraka for the 4H

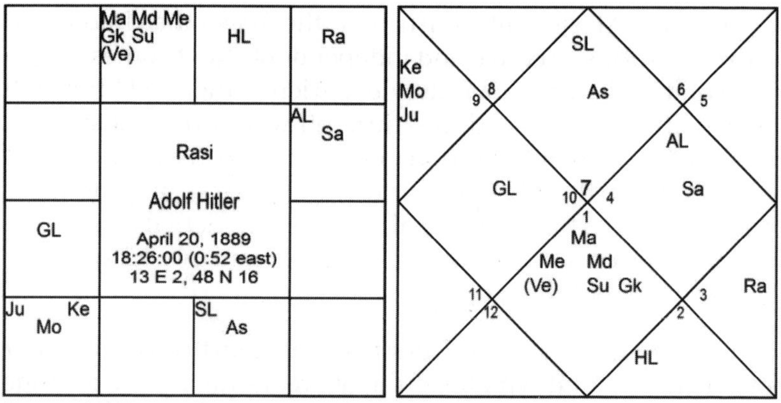

As:	3 Li 39	Su:	8 Ar 31- PK	Mo:	14 Sg 18- PiK	Ma:	24 Ar 06- AmK
Me:	3 Ar 23- DK	Ju:	15 Sg 57- MK	Ve (R):	24 Ar 24- AK	Sa:	21 Cn 10- BK
Ra:	22 Ge 48- GK	Ke:	22 Sg 48	HL:	18 Ta 05	GL:	18 Cp 13

– and also for his father as 2H from the 9H. In fact, his family had to move due to his father's work change and the father-son relationship was tensed at times due to Hitler's disregard for authorities despite being a bright student. Saturn also occupies the 4H of physical death from the Sun – his father passed away in January 1903 when Hitler was 13. Then came more unsettlement when he tried to be accepted as an artist but without success. After his mother's demise in 1907, the influence moved to another vantage point in his chart.

The next cycle up to his 36th year starts from the 9H in Gemini occupied by Rahu. Rahu is completed by 3 planets in the 7th House from its position in fiery and potentially fanatical Sagittarius – Ketu which is very militaristic, Jupiter which is very idealistic and Moon which represents the public. Moreover, 4 planets sit in the 11th House of gains from Rahu's position – Sun and Mars, both king and commander in chief with Mercury for speech and Venus the Lagna Lord, to add art and manipulation to the mix. All these are in Aries, the first sign of Kalapurusha which is fond of making strategies to conquer the perceived oppressors of freedom. Both 7H and 11H are kama houses and so, his views of the world could be said to be grounded in desires chan- nelled through his associates and attachments to gains, and moreover fuelled by ideologies.

To open a karmic parenthesis, we could add that from his JL Lord Venus, Rahu occupies the 3H, another kama house. Rahu in 3H shows unnatural attachments as the growth of his physical attachments i.e. the 7H from JL. Basically, from any trine, the themes of 3H, 7H and 11H are emphasized with lots of fire sign element – so passion rules. When we consider the 9H as JL for that second part of his life, Rahu shows unusual "self" expansion as a result of his men- tal attachments in Aries as 11H. Besides, Rahu occupies Gemini, sign of the twins who doubly fortifies his unstoppable impulse to grab and own all. Rahu occupies the 9H from JL which shows that this continues the activities of his previous birth. The JL Lord in 7H shows that 7H is spoiled and that he dug his own grave – end of this karmic parenthesis.

Anyways, at this point, all this karmic baggage was ripening up since this is when he fought in WWI, then worked as an intelligence agent for the army, and finally started working fulltime for the *National Socialist German Workers Party* where he became expert at giving speeches to large crowds. During this period he matured his Nazi ideology and wrote his *Mein Kampf,* Gemini representing communications.

The last cycle starts in the 5H, Aquarius. We are now in 1925 when he was published. He had to keep quiet until 1929 when the stock market crashed in the USA, event which badly troubled Germany's economy. The Lord of Aquarius is placed in the 6H from there, 6H being confrontations, competitions and war amongst others. From Lagna, this happens to be the 10H of one's actions in the world – and Saturn occupies the sign of Cancer which is the home and land in general. Cancer itself tends to inflate the sector of activities it represents. Moon the Lord of Cancer is with expansive and idealistic Jupiter and military Ketu in an all ambitious fire sign – therefore the mind is prone to utopias. These three occupy the 11H of gains, mental attachments and satisfaction of one's desires from Aquarius (mmmm....) Saturn in the 6H is also Lord of the 12H of losses from Aquarius while from Lagna, it is the 4th Lord of physical death.

Rahu occupies the 5H of politics and wisdom in the last part of his life showing growth and thirst for power. Also, Rahu being in Gemini home of the twins which is the 12H of loss from Cancer as the 6H seen from Aquarius, his country was left split in two parts with loss of territory and stripped of all its gains acquired during the war.

As for the 4 planets in Aries as the 3H of communications from Aquarius, they reinforced the militarism and idealism of his speech as already evident from natal Lagna. And so it was.

> Moon signifies mother/elder sister and Venus wife. When mother dies, Moon signifies the wife. If there should be another woman, she will be signified by Venus.
>
> * * * * * * * * *
>
> Moon and Mercury exchange: ill fame

Karakatwas As Applied In Nadi Combination of Planets

Just... Mix them!

Sun + Moon Father + variable mind

Father + mother shift from place of birth Ego + mother egoistical

Sun + Mars

Father + co-borns (father lives with co-borns) Separates + relatives

Separates + brother (1 brother lives with father) Separates + husband

Separates + job (leaves job 2 times) Government + husband (her husband works for the Government)

Government + uniform, profession (her spouse or herself wear a uniform in profession)

Separates & bones + marrow inside bone = separates bones to get to marrow = Sun + Mars will take revenge at all cost (break himself)

Sun + Mercury = good education Government + education

Father etc. + witty, talks, business

Sun + Jupiter = name & fame / well to do Father + good, fat

Permanent + jaundice

Sun + Venus = father rich and/or interested in women

Separates + 2nd sister

King + wife = she rules the house

Power + wife = wife arrogant Separates + wife

Hot + semen = dries sperm so can cause impotency

Sun + Saturn = father low paid Father + discipline

Atma + discipline

Father + losses = lost father or ego clash

Ego + restrictions = fights within himself / conflicted

Moon + Mercury & Mars + Jup are also conflicted within

Sun + Rahu = difficult times / worldly curse

Eye + obstruction

Father + obstruction = in filial love from dad Father + stranger = father away

Eye + defect Sun + Rahu

Father's marriage under compulsion

Moon + Rahu = marriage was mother's choice Sun + Ketu = religious / curse of a deity or deva / birth of child is tough Atma + religious

Jup + Ven + Mercury Deity beauty budhi = wife smart

Jiva sharing social = relation outside marriage

ROLE OF NAKSHATRAS & NAVAMSHA

LIFE STARTS IN THE DHARMA SIGNS

NAVAMSHA is the FRUIT of the RASI CHART and SHOWS if we GET WHAT the RASI PROMISED or NOT

SUN is ATMA and its first Nakshatra is the royal MAGHA. The deity for Magha is Pitur: forefathers.

JUPITER is JIVA with its starting Nakshatra as MULA ruled by Nirutti the dark demon associated with the womb. This is where Life comes out of the womb and breaks darkness... at last! The endless sky becomes the limit. Since all Jivas need energy, the next Dharma sign is ARIES where...

MARS is ENERGY! Its first Nakshatra is ASHWINI. The deity is the Ashwini Kumar which grants horse power.

"Moolatrikona" is composed of two words: "moola" being beginning of life – the name originates from Mula Nakshatra which is the origin – and "Trikona" as the trines 1, 5, 9.

As for the other moolatrikona rashis, we find them as the uppachaya rashis which are the growth rashis: 3, 6, 10, 11. For the Jiva to grow, these houses become the other planets moolatrikona rashi namely:

3H from Sagittarius is Aquarius, moolatrikona for Saturn

6H from Sagittarius is Taurus, moolatrikona for the Moon

10H from Sagittarius is Virgo, moolatrikona for Mercury

11H from Sagittarius is Libra, moolatrikona for Venus

SUN, JUPITER and MARS are all MALE PLANETS and they are PIVOTAL for the CHART and FIRST MOOLATRIKONA RASHI

3H is effort – viryasthana – linked to Saturn

6H is discrimination – for the Moon (inner mind from past life)

10H is karma activity – for Mercury 11H is friends, sharing – for Venus

Sun, Mars and Jupiter connect the rashis as follows:

Aries (fire) to Taurus (earth) connected by Sun Taurus (earth) to Gemini (Air) linked by Mars Gemini (Air) to Cancer (Water) by Jupiter From Water to Fire is the end of Life, the famous gandanta

Next, we'll be looking at Nakshatras from different angles...

The Nakshatra a planet occupies shows the real root or bio data – per example, with Moon in Sagittarius Purva Ashada, Venus' Nakshatra, besides the sharing aspect of Venus, the Moon will also perceive folks as being either enemies (6H in Taurus) or friends (11H in Libra). And if Moon goes to Virgo Navamsha (2nd pada of PA), there will necessarily be "enemies" to argue with.

See the Navamsha positions superposed with the natal position. In this perspective, the Navamsha positions should not go to the 6H or 8H from their natal position. Per example, if we take an Aries Lagna native with Mars in Gemini – and having Navamsha Mars conjunct Rahu in Capricorn... Navamsha Mars being in the 10H from Lagna, we could expect that this person's communications create conflicts and problems in the career. And if we consider that the Lord of a House in Navamsha Houses 6, 8 or 12 shows Fate from past actions, then we know the person from the example above has no choice to undergo unpleasant self-created situations...

Take the rasi of the natal 7H (per example Scorpio for Taurus JL). Now see that same 7H rasi (Scorpio here) in the Navamsha chart. If occupied by...

- Mercury shows divorce // if Mercury is found in 1H (i.e. Taurus here) the person would marry a "divorcee" i.e. not a virgin
- Moon signifies an older woman
- Sun as ego shows separation
- Jupiter indicates selfishness or the elder brother

If no planet occupies the Navamsha 7H, then one's marriage is not fated to be problematic. If big problems occur, it will be the couple's self-making.

Mars and Moon next to Rahu: his brothers and sisters will have to face some troubles

* * * * * * * * *

Moon placed in the 2nd house to Saturn: he will have friends dealing in chemicals

* * * * * * * * *

Venus and Saturn in Taurus: rich and prominent person

* * * * * * * * *

Jupiter and Venus in 6/8: separation from the wife for a short while

1st Scheme – Nakshatra Ownership From Each Sign

This table shows the underlying motivation of planets in the Nakshatra where they each land...

Sign	Sign Nakshatra Lords from there
ARIES	Ketu = owns no house and is 100% karma Venus = owns 2H & 7H = earning and relations Sun = owns 5H = children
TAURUS	Sun = owns 4H = domesticated Moon = owns 3H = short journeys (carried by the bull) Mars = owns 7H & 12H = partnerships & physical comfort
GEMINI	Mars = owns 6H & 11H = friends are enemies or vice versa Rahu = owns no house and is 100% karma – he is not what he looks like Jupiter = owns 7H & 10H = partnerships & profession / close to in-laws or aliens
CANCER	Jupiter = 6H & 9H = not good for relation with father Saturn = 7H & 8H = not happy for marriage & obtains public money Mercury = 3H & 12H = loss through neighbours
LEO	Ketu = 100% karma Venus = owns 3H & 10H = acting // 3H = unnatural attachment in 10H Sun = owns 1H (Mars as 4L & 9L shows mom & dad power)
VIRGO	Sun = owns 12H = sleep, liberation Moon = owns 11H = finances and gains Mars = owns 3H & 8H = unnatural attachment in 8H (mysteries...)

Jupiter in Leo: good looks (for a female)

* * * * * * * * *

Jupiter (native), Sun (father) with Venus between them: the relationship will not be cordial as Venus is an enemy of Jupiter

Sign	Sign Nakshatra Lords from there
LIBRA	Mars = owns 2H & 7H = earning, relations Rahu = 100% karma – is not what he looks like Jupiter = owns 3H & 6H = unnatural attachments in 6H (pets, diets...)
SCORPIO	Jupiter = owns 2H & 5H = good in advising others regarding finances Saturn = owns 3H & 4H = unnatural attachment in 4H (mother, info...) Mercury = owns 8H & 11H = public money and profits
SAGITTARIUS	Ketu = 100% karma Venus = owns 6H & 11H = share good & bad Sun = owns 9H = Bhagya of Jiva
CAPRICORN	Sun = owns 8H = public money, hidden things Moon = owns 7H = partnerships Mars = owns 4H & 11H = mother & landed property
AQUARIUS	Mars = owns 3H & 10H = acting // 3H = unnatural attachment in 10H Rahu = 100% karma – is not what he looks like Jupiter = owns 2H & 11H = hold on to money
PISCES	Jupiter = owns 1H & 10H = Jiva and his actions in the world Saturn = owns 11H & 12H = finances and expenses Mercury = owns 4H & 7H = education and partnerships --- End of all = cycle complete ---

2ND SCHEME – WHERE'S THE HOUSE LORD'S NAKSHATRAS?

Sign	Sign Lord Nakshatra placement from sign
ARIES	Mars = 2 – 6 – 10 // 3 – 7 – 11 = artha & kama i.e. attachments
TAURUS	Venus = 4 – 8 – 12 = moksha
GEMINI	Mercury = 2 – 6 – 10 = artha
CANCER	Moon = 3 – 7 – 11 = kama
LEO	Sun = 1 – 5 – 9 // 2 – 6 – 10 = dharma & artha
VIRGO	Mercury = 3 – 7 – 11 = kama
LIBRA	Venus = 3 – 7 – 11 = kama
SCORPIO	Mars = 3 – 7 – 11 = kama // 4 – 8 – 12 = moksha
SAGITTARIUS	Jupiter = 3 – 7 – 11 = kama // 4 – 8 – 12 = moksha
CAPRICORN	Saturn = 3 – 7 – 11 = kama
AQUARIUS	Saturn = 2 – 6 – 10 = artha
PISCES	Jupiter = 1 – 5 – 9 = dharma // 4 – 8 – 12 = moksha

This table refers to the position occupied by the Nakshatras owned by the Lord of the rashi from his rashi. It applies no matter which House a rashi happens to be.

For example, with Aries JL, since Mars' Nakshatras links two signs, artha and attachments would be underlying motivations of the person. Should Aries be the 2H (for Pisces Lagna), then the artha and attachments would be main players in this person's income, material acquisitions and recognition (2, 6, 10) while the mode of earning would be much influenced by factors of personal growth, harmony and attachment to the partner (3, 7, 11). Got it? So we can play with these and unearth hidden impetus...

3rd Scheme – Through Which Houses Are The Fate And Moksha Lords Operating?

The next table below shows where karma operates for each Lagna. All is based on trines. We will find the Houses where the House Lord's Nakshatras are placed from the House under observation (from the 6H for example) and see in which Houses from Lagna these Nakshatras land. Here's how to work this out:

First, the Fate "biggies" and our thinking free will

6H for Prarabdha: can't change it...

8H for what's hidden 12H for losses, expenses 4H for moksha

Second, the Houses where Fate could operate...

1, 5, 9 = Dharma so this karma operates on the self, one's child and one's father & ancestors

2, 6, 10 = Artha i.e. one's income and family, debts, litigations or the partner's happiness, career

3, 7, 11 = Kama, i.e. spiritual, physical or mental attachments – or one's second child, the younger and/or elder sibling, business, gains, friendship, etc.

4, 8, 12 = Moksha through one's conscious thoughts, one's hidden emotions or other people's money or one's private life, sleep, dreams and bed comforts

Note: please refer to our Bhavas section for more Houses' karakatwas.

For example, if we take Sagittarius Lagna, the 6H is

Taurus owned by Venus. So, the 6H Lord's Nakshatras occupy Houses 1, 5, 9 (fire signs) so we would say the 6H operates on the person or self.

For the 8H (Cancer), Moon operates on Houses 2, 6, 10 i.e. on artha so; one's income, work and actions would be influenced by others' money or litigations, hidden stuff, scandals, chronic illness, etc.

The 12H (Mars) operates on Houses 2, 6, 10 and 3, 7, 11 so on artha and kama: money, family, work and on one's attachments – these are the places where extra expenses and losses should be expected.

4H (Jup) operates on 3, 7, 11 and 4, 8, 12 so, moksha is obtained through attachments and all that relates to the mental functions either conscious, sub-conscious, the occult, mysteries, or meditation, ashrams, dreams... What this 4H moksha really means is that by applying our thinking conscious free will to these areas, we empower ourselves to take our own stance in life instead of taking a victim's position. Indeed, therein resides the duality between the human and animal parts of the Centaur as Sagittarius' symbol, Jiva's very home. Freedom and responsibility come hand in hand.

Lagna Rashi	Lord of...	Rashi	Houses where the Rashi's Nakshatras operate
ARIES	6H	Virgo	4, 8, 12
	8H	Scorpio	2, 6, 10 and 3, 7, 11
	12H	Pisces	3, 7, 11 and 4, 8, 12
	4H	Cancer	2, 6, 10
TAURUS	6H	Libra	4, 8, 12
	8H	Sagittarius	2, 6, 10 and 3, 7, 11
	12H	Aries	1, 5, 9 and 2, 6, 10
	4H	Leo	4, 8, 12 and 1, 5. 9

GEMINI	6H	Scorpio	1, 5, 9 and 4, 8, 12
	8H	Capricorn	2, 6, 10
	12H	Taurus	4, 8, 12
	4H	Virgo	2, 6, 10
CANCER	6H	Sagittarius	1, 5, 9 and 2, 6, 10
	8H	Aquarius	1, 5, 9
	12H	Gemini	1, 5, 9
	4H	Libra	2, 6, 10
LEO	6H	Capricorn	4, 8, 12
	8H	Pisces	3, 7, 11 and 4, 8, 12
	12H	Cancer	2, 6, 10
	4H	Scorpio	2, 6, 10 and 3, 7, 11
VIRGO	6H	Aquarius	3, 7, 11
	8H	Aries	1, 5, 9 and 2, 6, 10
	12H	Leo	1, 5, 9 and 4, 8, 12
	4H	Sagittarius	2, 6, 10 and 3, 7, 11
SCORPIO	6H	Aries	3, 7, 11 and 4, 8, 12
	8H	Gemini	1, 5, 9
	12H	Libra	2, 6, 10
	4H	Aquarius	4, 8, 12
SAGITTARIUS	6H	Taurus	1, 5, 9
	8H	Cancer	2, 6, 10
	12H	Scorpio	2, 6, 10 and 3, 7, 11
	4H	Pisces	3, 7, 11 and 4, 8, 12

CAPRICORN	6H	Gemini	3, 7, 11
	8H	Leo	1, 5, 9 and 4, 8, 12
	12H	Sagittarius	2, 6, 10 and 3, 7, 11
	4H	Aries	1, 5, 9 and 2, 6, 10
AQUARIUS	6H	Cancer	4, 8, 12
	8H	Virgo	2, 6, 10
	12H	Capricorn	2, 6, 10
	4H	Taurus	3, 7, 11
PISCES	6H	Leo	2, 6, 10 and 3, 7, 11
	8H	Libra	2, 6, 10
	12H	Aquarius	1, 5, 9
	4H	Gemini	1, 5, 9

Judging Of Charts According To Nadi Principles

In a natal chart, see the person first and then this person's relatives using their karakatwas planets (Sun for father etc.) and verify some past events.

See planets in house relations to each other. KENDRAS bring tensions – they can't balance each other since the sign elements clash. But then, Kendras are good for mundane activities. TRINES relations are relaxed and bring more happiness. They are said to be more "spiritual" or can just make one lazy to try something new since things flow on their own accord – some call it luck. One may thus be tempted to repeat the same experience.

HOUSES FROM ANYWHERE SHOW the OUTCOME of THAT HOUSE

- 4H shows the happiness of the House concerned
- 5H shows its purva punya
- 7H shows its complement
- 8H show longevity
- 9H shows its bhagya
- 10H shows its actions

Per example: marriage is 7H so the 2H (8H from 7H) shows its longevity, the 11H its purva punya (5H from 7H) while the 10H shows the happiness of the marriage partner (4H from the 7H of spouse).

The general rule is that any planets in the 2H, 12H, 7H and trines from a planet influence that planet positively or negatively. As all yogas depend on the Moon, if there are NO planets at all in 2/12 or 7H from Moon... other yogas may not fructify...!

If the planets in 2/12 and/or 7H are not friends, they will not allow each other to work and prosper – they will obstruct. In this condition, the planet we are examining will not be able to exhibit its full potential even if in its very own house. Therefore, if a planet is strong and good with unfriendly planets on its side houses, the others will stop it from giving good results but it need not give bad results. Of these, the 7H plays a bigger role of influence for better or for worse since the 7H is the completion... or death.

If a planet is weak with enemies in 2/12 then it will give bad results. For example, with Saturn in Aries damaged by the Moon in 2H and the Sun in 12H, the profession is very afflicted. If the planet afflicting in the 2H is retrograded, bad results are expected. If the planet afflicting in the 12H is retrograded then that is alright since it is going away. For example, if Saturn (the giver of profession) is retrograded and Jupiter (the self) is retrograded in the 12H from Saturn, the person runs away from profession. If Jupiter would be in the 2H from Saturn and retrograde, then this person would have to go for the job that comes to him or her.

An exalted planet with no support in 2/12 and/or 7H cannot perform whereas a fallen planet with friends in 2/12 can do something.

Here is an example...

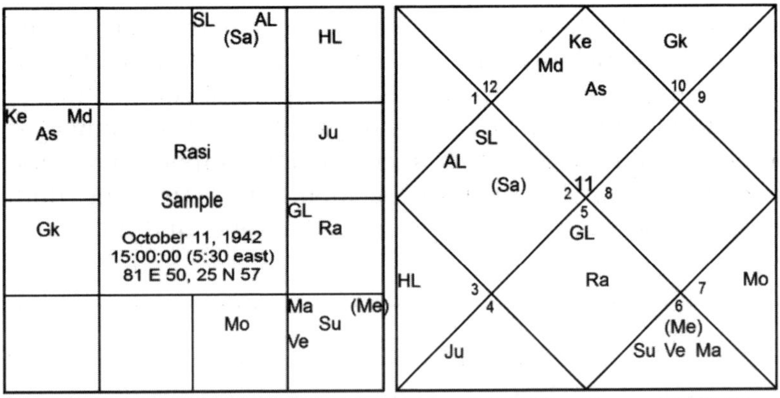

As:	1 Aq 45	Su:	24 Vi 24- AK	Mo:	10 Li 20- GK	Ma:	22 Vi 38- BK
Me (R):	23 Vi 40- AmK	Ju:	0 Cn 33- DK	Ve:	15 Vi 13- PK	Sa (R):	19 Ta 15- PiK
Ra:	10 Le 26- MK	Ke:	10 Aq 26	HL:	22 Ge 37	GL:	5 Le 30

Take Saturn for profession. As the planet for karma, activity, it has no planets on either side or in the 7H so nothing stopping and nothing helping. But there are 4 planets in the 5H from Saturn – this shows that his actions will be future oriented and their fruits will be seen in the future – so the Lords of Houses 3, 5, 7, 8, 9, 10 belong in that future.

The 2H from Saturn, domestic activity – Gemini here, is here ruled by Moon and Ketu in trikona so parents, grand-parents, in-laws or an elderly woman on the maternal side influence.

12H from Saturn has trikona Rahu so aliens, cinema would be significant – the push is given by outsiders who play the role in pushing his activity (Muslims, etc.)

Next take Jupiter for Jiva. As the planet for free will, it has Rahu in the 2H, no planet in the 12H and 7H and no planet in trikona showing that his desires and actions happen for the sake of the present. Jupiter and Rahu are not enemies so; they do not obstruct one another. Therefore what he does in the present, his choice, will reward him with Saturn i.e. his profession since Saturn occupies the 11H from Jupiter.

The 2H to Jiva, domestic activity and money earned, is Leo ruled by the Sun. Rahu sits there showing that aliens or other Rahu topics like esoterism or cinema, have some kind of influence over his free will as far as family life and his earnings are concerned. Ketu occupies, of course, the 7H from Rahu and so, his earnings would be complemented or obstructed by elements such as hot temper, something martial, losses, frustrations, accidents and surprises. Both Rahu and Ketu are related to grand-parents and out of the norm people and events.

> No planet between Rahu and Mars: death of brothers – see other planets in the same way for other relatives (use karakatwas)
>
> * * * * * * * * *
>
> Saturn placed in the 5th house to Venus: trouble with children

12H from Jupiter, Gemini, has trikona Moon and Ketu so parents, grand-parents, in-laws or an elderly woman on the maternal side influence – and Christians, something related to accidents or martial in nature, with also notions of illusions, personal fantasies, artists, etc. are driving forces behind his free will. And so on...

How to Use The Karakatwa Uccha and Neecha Rashi in Judgment

As mentioned earlier, for Uccha – or exalted – planets, their moolatrikona sign and the house they occupy depending on the Lagna will be affected. For example, for Sagittarius Lagna with Venus exalted in the 4H, Venus' sign of Libra occupies the 11H. This means the person's older sibling, or a friend, or the son/ daughter-in-law is likely to be found with some kind of defect or peculiar problems in life. The person's marriage or conjugal type relation could also prove to be irregular or unbalanced.

> An exchange of Venus and Mars grants an attractive personality
>
> * * * * * * * * * *
>
> Venus in Cancer: humiliations through a woman when Jupiter transits over Venus

A Neecha or fallen planet on the contrary is deemed good as the area of life it shows has not been developed in the past and the owner of such a planet will get outside help.

Example Lord Ramachandra

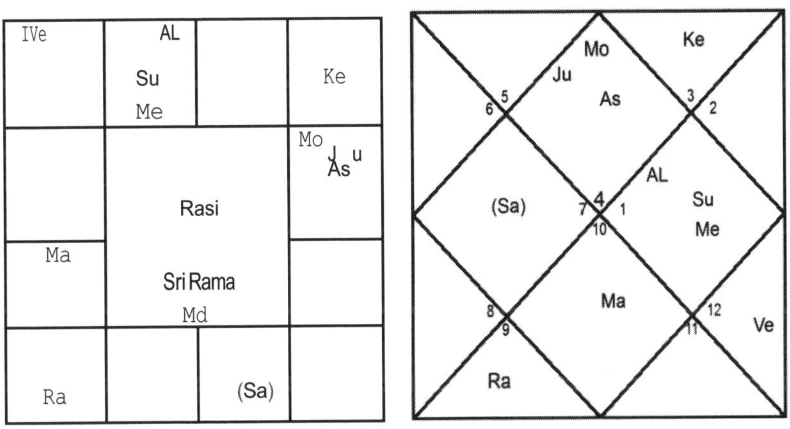

Problem areas:

Venus is exalted so Libra, the 4H of mother and domestic happiness has a problem.

Jupiter is exalted so Dhanur (Sag) as 6H enemies, wife's bed comforts...not happy.

Mars exalted so xoH: He coul rot rule His kingdom for 14 years and was separated from his children

i.e. Aries is 6H from the 5H. He even fought against His own sons!

Saturn is exalted so 8H – his wife has no family; she was born from the Earth.

Sun exalted so 2H i.e. some tensions in His family of birth, His food (He ate fruits in the forest – not a king's usual diet). Since His 2H is the 12H of his next born brother – Laxman (12H from 3H), His brother's bed comforts were destroyed.

> Saturn has no planet on either side and no planet in the 7th house from it: the native has to depend on others

Mars in Pisces for a female chart: the husband is highly educated

* * * * * * * * * * *

Venus in the 12th house to Jupiter: the native will have unhappy married life.
Troubles from females

Jupiter and Moon in Pisces: troubles for the mother at birth

* * * * * * * * *

Mercury and Mars exchanging houses: break in education, financial gains from brothers

* * * * * * * * *

Mars conjunct Rahu: interruptions in education and dogged nature

Session 2 – Dashas In Nadis

Three Divisions: Past, Present, Future – How To Work It Out

1- See the Major Vimshottari Dasha running.

2- Find the first Nakshatra of this planet starting from the Moon's position. Per ex- ample, for someone running Venus Dasha with natal Moon in Cancer, the first Venus Nakshatra is Purva Phalguni in Leo – all of Venus' Nakshatras occupy in fire signs.

3- The Dasha will be divided in 3 equal parts starting with its first Nakshatra position.

a. The first part refers to events and activities that are accomplished because of the past. No matter what the natal Lagna is, for reading the Dasha with our Venus example above, we will read the first 6 years and 8 months of the running Dasha from Leo as Lagna. Whatever we see happening from this vantage point would take place because of some past life repercussions.

b. The second part refers to events and activities that are accomplished because of the present. After those 6, 8 years, we read the Dasha from the next Venus Nakshatra which is Purva Ashada in Sagittarius. The events we can foresee from there should occur because of what the person needs to accomplish to deal with his/her present circumstances.

c. The third part refers to events and activities that are accomplished because of the future. After another 6, 8 years, the person's Dasha reading would move to the third Venus Nakshatra, Bharani in Aries. The life circumstances emerging from this perspective will take place because they are needed to lay the ground for what is to come in the future – whether one is aware of this or not.

Per example, someone obtains a new friend. If this would occur during the first third of the Dasha, we would say that this friend came at that time because of the past. If this friend would be made during the middle portion of the Dasha, this friend would appear because he is part of circumstances that must prevail in the present. Should this friend be encountered in the last third of the Dasha, then this friend is someone who had to be met for the sake of events yet to come.

Planets in 2nd house to Sun show father's earnings

* * * * * * * * *

Mars placed in the 2nd house to Sun: he will be in a hurry to do things

* * * * * * * * *

Saturn on one side of the Rahu/Ketu axis and Jupiter on the other: the native gets employed in a faraway place and struggles hard

* * * * * * * * *

Mercury in Lagna: native goes on pilgrimage at the age of 27

* * * * * * * * *

Moon in 2nd house to Venus denies female issues

Table of Divisions Starting With Nakshatra Lords

Dasha Lord	Dasha Period Length	Sub-Period Divided By 3	Sub - Sub-Period Sub-period divided by 12 Rashis
KETU	7 years	2 yrs 4 months each	2 months 10 days
Nakshatras	1 – Ashwini	10 – Magha	19 – Moola
VENUS	20 years	6 yrs 8 months each	6 months 20 days
Nakshatras	2 – Bharani	11 – Purva Phalguni	20 – Purva Ashada
SUN	6 years	2 yrs each	2 months
Nakshatras	3 – Krittika	12 – Uttara Phalaguni	21 – Uttara Ashada
MOON	10 years	3 yrs 4 months each	3 months 10 days
Nakshatras	4 – Rohini	13 – Hasta	22 - Shravana

Dasha Lord	Dasha Period Length	Sub-Period Divided By 3	Sub - Sub-Period Sub-period divided by 12 Rashis
MARS	7 years	2 yrs 4 months each	2 months 10 days
Nakshatras	5 – Mrigashira	14 – Chitra	23 – Danishta
RAHU	18 years	6 yrs each	6 months
Nakshatras	6 – Ardra	15 – Swati	24 – Shatabhishak
JUPITER	16 years	5 yrs 4 months each	5 months 10 days
Nakshatras	7 – Punarvasu	16 – Vishaka	25 – Purva Bhadrapada
SATURN	19 years	6 yrs 4 months each	6 months 10 days
Nakshatras	8 – Pushya	17 – Anuradha	26 – Uttara Bhadrapada
MERCURY	17 years	5 yrs 8 months each	5 months 20 days
Nakshatras	9 – Ashlesha	18 – Jyestha	27 - Revati

As shown in these tables, each of the Dasha's 3 divisions can further be divided into 12 sub-sub-periods. So, each sub-sub-period would be progressed through each rashi using its own time frame and starts at the same time and in the same sign as the sub-period rashi.

For the connectivity Nakshatras i.e. Sun, Jupiter and Mars, as these spread over two rashis, the two houses they will be involved with from our starting point should be considered as interconnected in the results. For example, starting from Leo, the Sun's Nakshatra will occur in both the 9H and 10H (Aries and Taurus) so the person could complete his or her higher education and obtain a job or start practicing a profession.

Moon Progressions Back & Forth Synchronized

Moon shows our past. Backward and forward progressions show how our present is connected to our past.

How to work it out:

1- Take the natal Moon's position.
2- Simultaneously progress the Moon forward and backward one house per year.
3- Since a picture is worth one thousand words, see the diagram below...

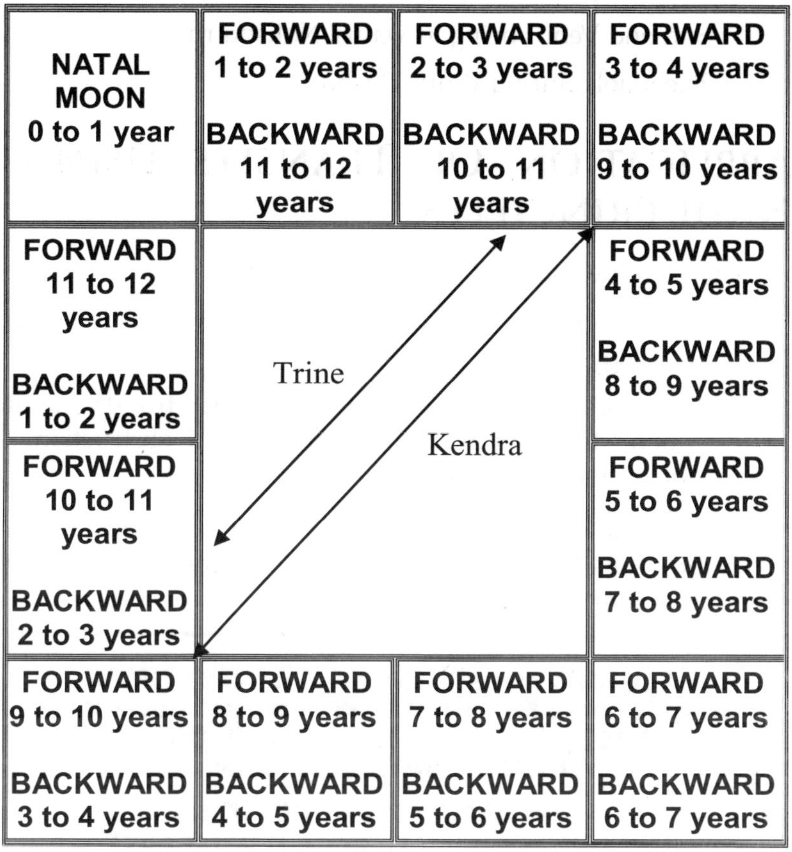

1- Trine and Kendra positions by progression show that the happenings of that year have to do with the past life i.e.

they are not the result of something done in this very life. The houses, grahas and Nakshatras involved will show in more detail.

Example: Heart attack. It happened when both Moon progressions involved:

- The 5H (physical heart) in Aries holding Ketu & Saturn in trine to Sun, Venus (6th Lord) and Mercury in the 9H, Leo
- Natal Rahu being in the 3H (blood) from the 9H

- Sun and Venus being in Venus' Nakshatra
- The whole during Venus Dasha

Application Of Transits Using Nadi Principles

There are two kinds of transits to consider:

1- The regular planetary transits used in mundane astrology which apply to all.

2- Gocharas which are the transits reckoned from the natal Moon – these should be seen in terms of obstruction – not as to what could be gained.

Transits play a role in the timing of events – like the hidden joker, they can obstruct a predictable event from taking place even if the chart is strong.

SATURN's transit gives FATE. JUPITER's transit gives FREE WILL. We can get our wish i.e. FREE WILL when transit JUPITER is in TRINE to NATAL SATURN.

When transit SATURN is in TRINE to NATAL JUPITER, we need to accept what FATE wants for us

By superposing the transits over a natal chart, see which planet produces a given change – if Saturn shows the event then it was fated whereas Jupiter giving the event indicates our own doing.

Rahu and Ketu, the 100% karma axis, bring us unavoidable and somehow deserved events right out of the blue. Ketu shows obstructions while Rahu can generously supply us with problems to manage and live with as well as positive rewards should we be eligible.

Venus conjunct Ketu: siddhi in mantra shastra or dealings in medicines.

One's wife may have mental troubles

Transit Jupiter and Saturn in 6/8 to their natal positions will bring the fall of something. Per example, losing one's position after a scandal. Jupiter and Saturn in 2/12 position show a lesser fall – Ex: to resign from a job after some problems in the environment.

For planning an activity, see the karakas involved at the time of the event as positioned over the natal chart. Per example, for giving a lecture – see Moon (internal mind) and Mercury (external mind) – they should not be in 6/8 from natal positions on the day planned.

Sun in the 3rd house from Saturn: influence in government.

Check planets in the 3rd house to Saturn for their influence as planets

* * * * * * * * *

No planet in the 7th house to Jupiter, Lagna and Lagna Lord: the native is "self-made"

i.e. not dependant on others

When a planet comes over a house or sign by transit, Nature's wish prevails. Per example, with Mars coming in the Sun's house, one may lose a brother (the Sun and the sign of Leo both separate from karakas involved with them).

Check Saturn's transit over natal Mars for accidents

* * * * * * * * *

Venus in the 12th house to Jupiter: the present wife is also his wife in the previous birth i.e. the 12H shows the last birth

Saturn's transits help us realize why we suffer. Per example, Saturn over one of our kama houses – places of attachments – has the potential of showing us the true value of our attach- ments. If transit Saturn as- pects the Lagna lord, it will surely bring restrictions.

Rahu placed next to Jupiter: wind troubles and nervous weakness

* * * * * * * * *

Transit Jupiter over natal Saturn: one may obtain a new job or promotion!

Session 3 – Advanced Level: Brighu

Metonic Cycle of Planets Used In Brighu Pada Dasha

Find below the total cycles for seven grahas – Rahu and Ketu are not considered in this scheme. After some explanations on the next page, the detailed breakdown of all these is provided to facilitate their use.

SUN = 19 years – 1 year, 7 months per sign MOON = 45 years – 3 years, 9 months per sign MERCURY = 46 years – 3 years, 10 months per sign

VENUS = 27 years – 2 years, 3 months per sign MARS = 14 years – 1 year, 2 months per sign JUPITER = 83 years – 6 years, 11 months per sign

SATURN = 30 years – 2 years, 6 months per sign

> Mercury conjunct Ketu: he tends to worry too much

Arudhas In Brighu Pada Dasha

How to find Arudhas

Count so many signs from the lord of a sign as the lord is away from its sign placement. Example: Lagna is Aquarius, Saturn is in Gemini. So the distance from the Lagna (Aq) to Saturn is 5 signs. By counting 5 signs from Gemini we land Libra. So the 9th House will be the Arudha Lagna (AL).

This same process can be applied to find the Arudha of every house.

There are exceptions applicable to the above rule known as "The Fourth House Rule":

If the lord of a house is in the 1st, 4th, 7th or 10th house, four houses must be deducted from the result.

Examples:

- Saturn occupies Aquarius Lagna. So the Lagna's Arudha (or AL) will not be Aquarius but Scorpio (or the 10H – that is, Lagna minus 4 houses – we counted backwards).
- The 4th house Arudha for Gemini Lagna with Mercury in Pisces: Gemini will be the Arudha and not Virgo (we subtracted 4 houses from Virgo, the 4H).

Note: The Arudha of the 12th house is known as Upapada Lagna (UL). All others can be referred to as "A2" for 2H Arudha, "A3" for 3H Arudha, etc. For the Lagna we use "AL".

The Lord of the House where the Arudha lands is that Arudha's *Control Planet*. For example, for Scorpio Lagna with the Arudha in Pisces, Jupiter becomes the *Control Planet* for the Lagna and is worth watching for all that concerns the Lagna. Accordingly, the Brighu Pada Dasha of Jupiter will be considered as the Lagna's Pada Dasha.

The following table gives the breakdown of the Pada Dasha's for all planets. These Pada Dasha's will shift houses from the position of the Dasha Lord at the pre-determined age. All Dasha's run simultaneously...!

Rahu is the grand-father. Mercury and Venus in the house next to Rahu indicate that the grand-father had wealth and landed property

METONIC CYCLE DASHA'S

Metonic Cycle Breakdown i.e. Pada Dashas Table

Houses→ Planets ↓	1 YY MM	2 YY MM	3 YY MM	4 YY MM	5 YY MM	6 YY MM	7 YY MM	8 YY MM	9 YY MM	10 YY MM	11 YY MM	12 YY MM
SUN	1-07	3-02	4-09	6-04	7-11	9-06	11-01	12-08	14-03	15-10	17-05	19
	20-07	22-02	23-09	25-04	26-11	28-06	30-01	31-08	3340	34-10	36-05	38
	39-07	41-02	42-09	44-04	45-11	47-06	49-01	50-08	52-03	53-10	55-05	57
	58-07	60-02	61-09	63-04	64-11	66-06	68-01	69-08	71-03	72-10	74-05	76
MOON	3-09	7-06	11-03	15-00	18-09	22-06	26-03	30-00	33-09	37-08	41-03	45
	48-09	52-06	56-03	60-00	63-09	67-06	71-03	75-00	78-09	82-06	86-03	90
MERCURY	3-10	7-08	11-06	15-04	19-02	23-00	26-10	30-08	34-06	38-04	41-02	46
	49-10	53-08	57-06	61-04	65-02	69-00	72-10	76-08	80-06	84-04	88-02	92
VENUS	2-03	4-06	6-09	9-00	11-03	13-06	15-09	18-00	2048	22-06	24-09	27
	29-03	31-06	33-09	36-00	38-03	40-06	42-09	45-00	47-03	49-06	51-09	54
	56-03	58-06	60-09	63-00	65-03	67-06	69-09	72-00	74-03	76-06	78-09	81

Houses→ Planets ↓	1 YY MM	2 YY MM	3 YY MM	4 YY MM	5 YY MM	6 YY MM	7 YY MM	8 YY MM	9 YY MM	10 YY MM	11 YY MM	12 YY MM
MARS	1-02	2 - 0 4	3-06	4 - 0 8	5-10	7-00	8 - 0 2	9 - 0 4	10-06	11-08	12-10	14
	15-02	16-04	17-06	18-08	19-10	21-00	22-02	234M	24-06	25-08	26-10	28
	29-02	30-04	31-06	32-08	33-10	35-00	36-02	37-04	38-06	39-08	40-10	42 56
	43-02	44-04	45-06	46-08	47-10	49-00	50-02	51-04	52-06	53-08	54-10	70
	57-02	58-04	59-06	60-08	61-10	63-00	64-02	65-04	66-06	67-08	68-10	84
	71-02	72-04	73-06	74-08	75-10	77-00	78-02	79-04	80-06	81-08	82-10	
JUPITER	6-11	13-10	20-09	27-08	34-07	41-06	48-05	55-04	62-03	69-02	76-01	83
SATURN	2 - 0 6	5 - 0 0	7 - 0 6	10-00	12-06	15-00	17-06	20-00	22-06	25-00	27-06	30 60
	32-06	35-00	37-06	40-00	42-06	45-00	47-06	50-00	52-06	55-00	57-06	90
	62-06	65-00	67-06	TWO	72-06	75-00	77-06	804M	82-06	85-00	87-06	

The Pada Dasha's starting point is the natal position of the *Control Planet* who becomes the Dasha Lord himself who becomes the venerable "House 1". He will be progressed forward, one house per age section. The climate of the periods will be viewed in reference to the Dasha Lord's position – or House 1 – as follows:

- Trines show that things will happen without the native asking for it
- Kendras indicate that there will be tensions and conflicts and the native will have to work for the desired results
- 6/8 positions show struggle and obstacles
- In 2/12 positions, the themes of one of the houses concerned will dominate over the other
- 3/11 positions show that the actions and their results flow in a complementary direction i.e. air-fire complete one another and water-earth also – so these positions can prove profitable (... depending on the actions!)

METONIC CYCLE SUB-DASHA'S

(The ", 5" days are approximations – could be ", 6")

SUN	MOON	MERCURY	VENUS
1 month & 6 days	3 months & 7, 5 days	3 months & 8, 5 days	2 months & 2, 5 days

MARS	JUPITER	SATURN
1 month & 1, 5 days	6 months & 27, 5 days	2 months & 15 days

This follows the same principle as done with the "sub-sub-period" of the Dasha's divided in three parts for past, present and future seen above. Therefore, each Sub-Dasha will start from the current Dasha's house position – and will be progressed forward using the time frames given so as to cover the twelve rashis.

Per example, for the 30, 8 years old native below with Aquarius Lagna and Saturn in the 4H, AL occupies the 4H itself (Taurus). So, the Lagna's *Control Planet* becomes Venus here placed in Virgo.

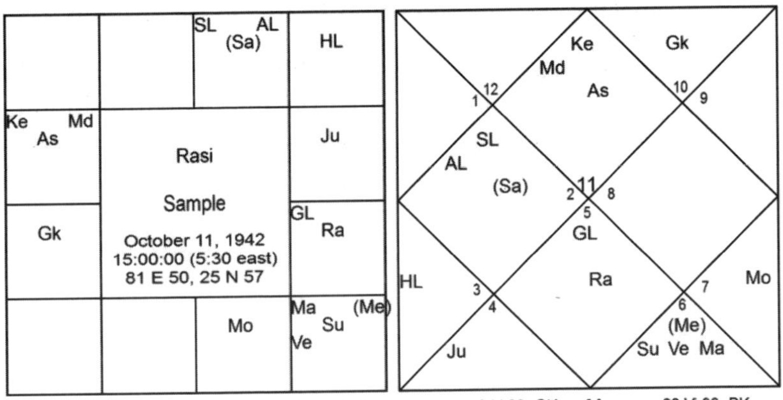

As:	1 Aq 45	**Su:**	24 Vi 24- AK	**Mo:**	10 Li 20- GK	**Ma:**	22 Vi 38- BK
Me (R):	23 Vi 40- AmK	**Ju:**	0 Cn 33- DK	**Ve:**	15 Vi 13- PK	**Sa (R):**	19 Ta 15- PiK
Ra:	10 Le 26- MK	**Ke:**	10 Aq 26	**HL:**	22 Ge 37	**GL:**	5 Le 30

Virgo becomes House 1. For a 30, 8 years old native, the Pada Dasha occurs in Libra the 2H from Venus between the ages of 29, 3 and 31, 6 years – as Libra is 9H from JL, he got married during this period. Now, the sub-dashas of 2 months and 2, 5 days also started running at 29, 3 years. Since a period of 8 months has elapsed by age 30, 8 the sub-dasha had covered 3 full signs and occupies the sign of Sagittarius, the 11H (of marriage) on the day of his wedding. So be it.

A7 which is also controlled by Venus in the same manner occupied the very same position as AL.

> For a female chart with Mars conjunct Rahu in Aquarius: when Saturn transits Aquarius, there will be troubles to the partner

Bhava Dasha

This one is all pre-determined. The elements used are:

- 8 planets out of which Rahu and Ketu are considered as one
- 12 houses
- 96 dashas are given. A planet will give its effect in specific year(s) according to its House position

In the table below, you will find that info goes mission for some planets – it got lost in the course of Time or, in translation...

> For Saturn conjunct Ketu in Mars' sign (Aries or Scorpio): the profession is connected with machines
>
> * * * * * * * * *
>
> Any planets in the 4H can't make a poor person rich or a rich person poor as can be the case with planets in the 10H
>
> * * * * * * * * *
>
> Saturn in trine to Venus: happy marriage

Years of Fructification in Houses

SUN		MOON		MARS		MERCURY	
House —	Year(s)	House —	Year	House —	Year	House —	Year
1 —	3rd	1 —	15th	1 —	5th	1 —	17th
2 —	25th	2 —	18th	2 —	13th	2 —	15th
3 —	4th, 5th, 8th, 12th	3 —	24th	3 —	__	3 —	25th
4 —	32nd	4 —	11th	4 —	8th	4 —	16th
5 —	7th	5 —	19th	5 —	6th	5 —	13th
6 —	20th	6 —	36th	6 —	27th	6 —	30th
7 —	25th	7 —	32nd	7 —	__	7 —	24th
8 —	10th	8 —	5th	8 —	24th	8 —	25th
9 —	_(14)	9 —	21st	9 —	17th	9 —	21st
10 —	18th	10 —	27th	10 —	18th	10 —	28th
11 —	25th	11 —	50th	11 —	23rd	11 —	20th
12 —	36th	12 —	29th	12 —	42nd	12 —	38th

YEARS OF FRUCTIFICATION IN HOUSES (2)

JUPITER	VENUS	SATURN	RA/KE
House — Year(s)	**House — Year**	**House — Year**	**House — Year**
1 — 16th	1 — 13th	1 — 4th	1 — 6th
2 — 16th	2 — 32nd	2 — 39th	2 — 13th
3 — 38th	3 — 19th	3 — 11th	3 — 9th
4 — 21st	4 — 30th	4 — __	4 — 17th
5 — 18th	5 — 24th	5 — 19th	5 — 21st
6 — 27th	6 — 31st	6 — 27th	6 — 28th
7 — 34th	7 — 12th	7 — __	7 — 5th
8 — __	8 — 4th	8 — 32nd	30th
9 — 35th	9 — 35th	9 — 16th	8 — 36th
10 — 32nd	10 — 39th	10 — 25th	9 — 45th
11 — 32nd	11 — 45th	11 — __	10 — 16th
12 — 45th	12 — 1st	12— 22nd,	11 - 43rd
		61st	12- 48th

SOME EVENTS TO EXPECT ACCORDING TO HOUSE POSITION

(Please note that these are not available for all years)

SUN	SUN	MOON	MOON
House — Year(s)	**House — Year(s)**	**House — Year**	**House — Year**
1 - 3rd Fever	6 - 20th Bad for eye	1 - 15th Travels	6 - 36th Widow connection
2 - 25th Government punishment	7 - 25th Travels	2 - 18th Government job	7 - 32nd Sex with women
3 - 4th, 5th 8th, 12th Bad years	8 - 10th Injury	3 - 24th Loss due to Government punishment	10 - 27th Widow connection
4 - 32nd Good years	10 - 18th Earns $$	4 - 11th Widow connection	11 - 25th Loss of children
5 - 7th Bad for father	11 - 25th Vehicles		
	12 - 36th Health upset		

SOME EVENTS TO EXPECT ACCORDING TO HOUSE POSITION (2)

MARS	MERCURY	MERCURY	VENUS
House — Year(s)	**House — Year**	**House — Year**	**House — Year**
4 - 8th Bad for father 5 - 6th Injury 6 - 27th Marriage with virgin 7 - _ 10- 18th Earns $$	1 - 27th Pilgrimage 2 - 15th Learns a lot 3 - 16th Gets a child 4 - 16th Profitable 6 - 3rd Increase friends	7 - 21st Good 8 - 28,h Child 9 - 21st 10- 28th Eye defect 11 - Good after 16th year	4 - 30th House construction 8 - 4th Throat trouble to mother

SOME EVENTS TO EXPECT ACCORDING TO HOUSE POSITION (3)

JUPITER	JUPITER	SATURN	GENERAL
House — Year(s)	**House — Year**	**House — Year**	
1 - 16th Government honour 2 - 16th Loss through thief 3 - 38th Pilgrimage 5 - 18th Government favour to father	7 - 34th Bad year 8-17th Widow connection 9 - 35th Homa,yagna 11 - 32nd Vehicles	9 - 39th Builds cow shelter (Does social service) 10- 25th Bathes in the Ganges	Sun in the 7H: will be deserted by husband Any planet in the 3H fructifies

NAISARGIKA – YEARS RULED BY PLANET(S)

Another pre-determined timing system. The years shift on the birthday. Per example, when one turns 4 years, Mars' influence starts and, on the 8th birthday, the influence shifts to Mercury. The table ends at 83 years so, for the 84th birthday, we start again with the Moon for the same number of years, then Mars, etc.

PLANET	YEARS RULING
MOON	1, 2, 3 years
MARS	4, 5, 6, 7 years
MERCURY	8, 9, 10, 11 years
VENUS	12, 13, 14, 15 years
JUPITER	16, 17, 18, 19, 20, 21 years
SUN	22, 23 years
MOON/VENUS	24, 25, 26, 27 years
MARS	28, 29, 30, 31 years
MERCURY	32, 33, 34, 35 years
SATURN	36, 37, 38, 39, 40, 41 years
RAHU	42, 43, 44, 45 years
MOON/RAHU	46, 47 years
Planet	Years ruling
SUN/MOON	48, 49, 50, 51 years
MARS	52, 53, 54, 55 years
JUPITER	56, 57, 58, 59 years

PLANET	YEARS RULING
VENUS	60, 61, 62, 63 years
MERCURY	64, 65, 66, 67 years
SATURN	68, 69, 70, 71 years
RAHU	72, 73, 74, 75, 76, 77 years
KETU	78, 79, 80, 81, 82, 83 years

With Moon in the 7th house to Mercury: blemish to the mother

* * * * * * * * *

Jupiter with Mercury in the 7th house and Venus in the 8th indicate two sources of happiness

* * * * * * * * *

Sun & Moon within the Nodes: no help from parents

SESSION 4 – YOGAS & PAST LIVES

The following is an excerpt from an article published by Saptarishi Astrology Magazine in 2011 titled "Yogas & Past Life – In Conversation with Mr. Sundaram". The whole article includes several more Yogas.

RUCHAKA YOGA

If Saturn aspects Mars there is no Yoga. Ruchaka yoga comes in this life since you previously took care of your brother. If you de- serted your brother in the last life, then in this life there will be Yoga Bhanga (Saturn's aspect).

Remedy: Should there be Yoga Bhanga then help others in a brother-like manner and Saturn should give the benefic results of Ruchaka Yoga.

BHADRA YOGA

If Mercury becomes paapi (Lord of a malefic house or afflicted with kendradipathi dosha) and is aspected by either of the 6th, 8th or 12th Lords, then Yoga Bhanga occurs. For a Virgo Lagna, Mercury is not paapi as 10L and Lagna Lord. For Gemini JL, Merc is a paapi i.e. Kendradipathi dosha. In such condition, if Merc is also aspected by one of 6th, 8th or 12th Lords, both conditions are fulfilled.

Past Life: You taught your disciples what you have learnt, then in this life you get Bhadra Yoga. If you die without teaching, then it's a Yoga Bhanga.

Remedy: In this life teach what you have learnt, teaching with open heart in guru-shishya context. Sharing is different: you share with equals.

HAMSA YOGA

If Jupiter becomes a paapi and joins a paapi, that's a Yoga Bhanga. The exception here is if Guru aspects those paapi's. When Guru joins them, one obtains Yoga Bhanga but when Jupiter aspects them, these paapi's will give the results of the Hamsa Yoga. This means that

Jupiter transfers on them the power of the result of this yoga, with his 5 or 9 aspects – not 7th. Paapi for Jupiter means from Mithuna or Kanya Lagnas or as Lord of 6, 8, or 12 houses. Malefics in 5H or 9H from Jupiter will have the power to give the yoga – Jupiter transfers the results of this yoga to them.

Past Life: He has constructed a Shiva Temple and he got the yoga. If he has taken the Shiva Temple property then Yoga Bhanga applies.

Remedy: If you can't give the property back to whom it belonged, then do service to the temple.

Another example: A native obtained a perfect Hamsa Yoga with no aspect of Saturn-Ketu or paapi's – but his Guru is vakri. This shows he has some left-over work from his past life. Additionally, Guru is vakri in the constellation of Shani. Shani should aspect according to the Bhanga rule. So, he is now doing his left-over work by serving in a Shiva temple. Though his chart does not show any Yoga Bhanga, because Guru is vakri, in his last life, he should have done this – that means there should have been Yoga Bhanga in his last life. That's why Jupiter occupies the constellation of Shani which is also vakri. So, if a planet is vakri and in the constellation of a vakri Lord, then both have direct relationship with the past life.

MALAVAYA YOGA

For Shukra, if Mars aspects then Yoga Bhanga occurs.

Past Life: You obtain Malavaya yoga since you have taken care of your wife properly in the past life. If you beat, scold, ill-treat your wife you get Yoga Bhanga. Even if Shukra is yogakaraka, the yoga will not grant results.

Suppose one possesses a fine Malavaya yoga with Shukra

as yogakaraka – if he ill-treats the wife in this very life the good results of this yoga will not manifest – though it refers to the with past life. If anything from the past is repeated here, the effect is felt. Same applies for the effects of all yogas given here.

Remedy: take good care of one's wife, that's all. (We can't say take care of others' wives... Shukra is basically one's wife – other significations such as younger sister etc. were not given here).

SASA YOGA

If you took care of your servants in the past life then Sasa Yoga is obtained in this life. When Mars aspects Saturn, Yoga Bhanga occurs. Why Mars? For all karma, Saturn, Rahu and Mars are the planets showing the past life effects. Mars is our energy right? And Saturn is the 3L (from Sagittarius, Jiva's moolatrikona).

To change our Fate we loop up to the 3H which is the reason why Saturn is given. Rahu's past life effect is due to its constant vakri motion. So Bhanga here shows that in the last life, the person did hurt servants.

Remedy: Take care of servants.

SUNAPA YOGA

Planets occupy the 2nd house from the Moon except the Sun.

Intelligent, self-earning in good ways without cheating others in the course of the earning activities. The Sun placed in the 2nd house to the Moon show that one earned in wrong ways in the past life. With such a Sun position, the astrologer should guide this native to avoid earning in wrong ways to keep suffering away – that is the message of this yoga.

ANAPA YOGA

Any planet in the 12th house to the Moon except the Sun.

He is famous, well placed and wealthy in life, with a body free from diseases and some frustration in the later part of life. In the last life, whatever he earned he spent in charity and dharmic activities. If the Sun occupies the 12H from the Moon, he spent in wrong ways.

Remedy: spend money for charitable purposes.

DURDHARA YOGA

Moon with planets in the 2nd and 12th houses from it except the Sun: a combination of the two yogas above.

KEMUDRUMA YOGA

The Moon having no planets on either side. Aspiring for others' property and giving pain to others in the past life is the reason for this yoga in this life. No specific remedy was given as these Bhanga's mean "don't do it".

VESI YOGA

Planets in the 2nd house to the Sun except the Moon.

Good education, good position. Even if he doesn't have wealth, he is helping others out of good heart despite the fact that he may not have sufficient wealth – this is the good karma for which he has gotten this yoga.

VASHI YOGA

Planets in the 12th house to the Sun except for the Moon.

Good wealth, good children. Just keeping his own earnings, leaving his father's property to others, getting the blessings of elders in the past life. If one has Moon in the 12th house to the Sun, he will suffer if he takes the father's property for himself now.

UBHAYACHARI YOGA

Planets in houses 2 and 12 to the Sun except for the Moon.

Atma balam, good food, good sleep. Staying with one's father, taking care of parents' sukha dukha in past life, one obtains this yoga in this life. Anyone with this yoga should be advised to take care of their father to avoid spoiling this fine yoga.

SUBHA KARTARI YOGA

The Sun conjunct with benefic planets and benefics occupying the houses on both sides of Sun.

He is a prophet, a vaidya, good person. In the past life, he has taken care of the father- in-law like one's own father hence this good yoga is granted. So one with this yoga should be advised to take care of his father to continue the yoga to avoid suffering that would result from neglect. This auspicious activity should be continued life after life. If malefics are present instead, then Yoga Bhanga occurs like in the next yoga...

PAPAKARTARI YOGA

Both sides of the Sun having paapi's.

Cleverly doing sins, fighting with enemies and insulting parents, one obtains this yoga.

Remedy: Fast on every Amavasya.

Venus – Moon opposition: loss of mother before marriage or ill health to the mother before marriage

* * * * * * * * *

Jupiter & Mars opposition: unhappy married life

* * * * * * * * *

Venus & Saturn conjunction: the native has misfortunes in life depending on the house where they are conjunct

Session 5 – Remedial Measures

Like a medicine, they are needed to remove those sufferings that occur due to one's karma and also others' actions.

Remedies – Man suffers because of:

3 doshas: Vata, Pitta, Kapha 3 kophas: anger

3 sabhas: curse

3 DOSHAS

KAPHA is ruled by the Moon. As it changes its shape due to the environment, by changing surroundings one can get sick ex: children. Attachments exist mentally so the Moon shows desires which are the cause of suffering.

PITTA (bile) is ruled by the Sun. Problems occur here due to individual actions, due to arrogance or ego: edging God out.

VATA is ruled by Saturn. Old age, blaming, back-biting, mischievous... All these are represented by the 6H.

Causes of suffering in a snapshot...

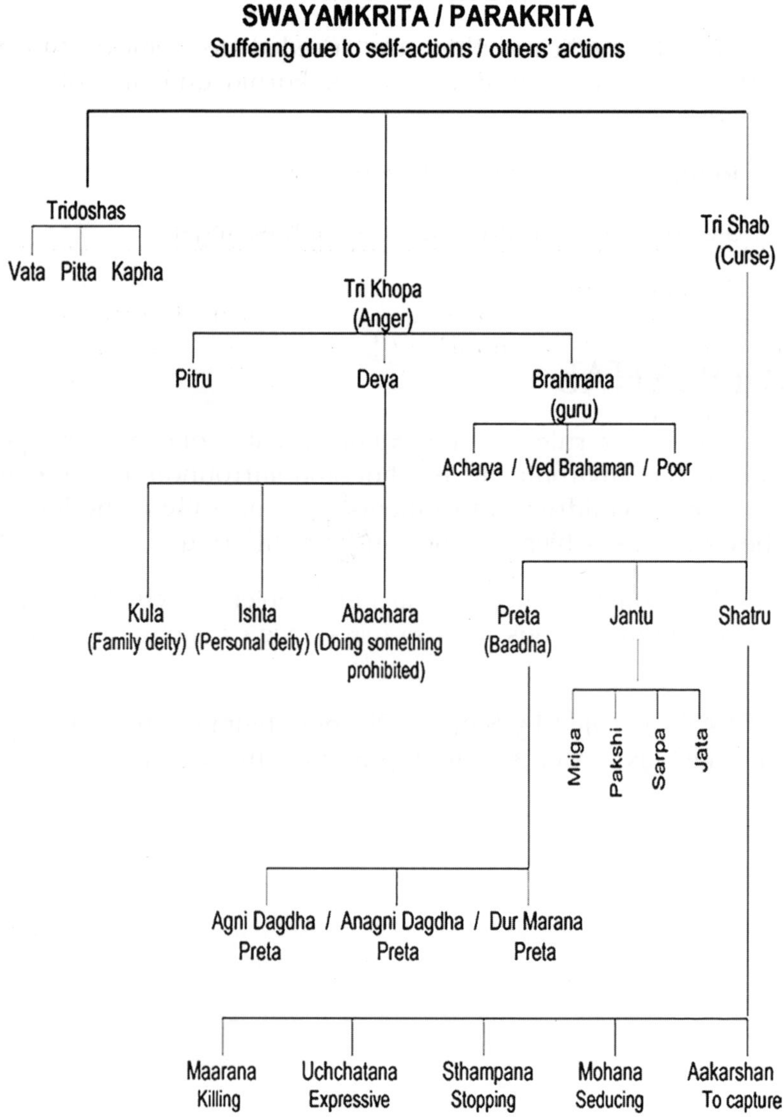

3 KOPHAS

Anger of PITUR: forefathers and elders by not obeying them, not performing duties for elders.

Anger of DEVA: deities, kula devata and/or personal deity due to not performing proper rituals to the deities... All these are indicated by the 8H.

Anger of GURU: guru, Brahmins by insulting scholars, teachers and poor Brahmins.

3 SABHAS

PRETA: dead persons by not paying respect to known or unknown dead bodies.

JANTU: animals, (birds, snakes, etc.) and living things – do not harm or kill them.

SHATRU: enemies – suffering due to enemy actions like black magic activities... All these are shown by the 12H.

One has to assert the intensity of suffering through the birth chart, dashas, gocharas and also a prashna made at the time of judging.

It remains beyond the scope of this presentation to supply further guidelines for giving remedies.

Session 6 – Prashna

1- A prashna chart could be made by taking a transit chart for the time of enquiry i.e. the birth of a question

2- Take a number between 1 to 108 (Nadiamshas) and divide by 9 to locate the Lagna

3- Take a number from 1 to 27 (Nakshatras) 4- Or a number between 1 to 12 for rashi

4- Or, open a book and see the page number – right page for him and left page for her. Divide the number by 108, or 27, or 12 as the case may be and fix the Lagna

5- Or, take the time shown on a watch – the hours indicate the Lagna, the minutes the position of the Moon

The prashna chart and native charts must have some similarity like prashna Moon in trine to natal Moon – or the prashna house dealing with the question is prominently exhibited.

Ex: question about the 5H has the 5th

Lord exalted in the prashna chart or the Moon occupies the prashna 5H.

With prashna used for remedial purposes to remove any trouble or sickness, locate the house(s) related to the problem.

For predictions about the future, go to the dashas and gocharas of both the natal and prashna charts.

In case of difficulty in identifying the problem in the natal chart, planets in 6 – 8 – 12 of the prashna chart should be taken as guidance for judging.

Moon placed in the 2nd house to Saturn: he will have friends dealing in chemicals

* * * * * * * * *

Venus and Saturn in Taurus: rich and prominent person

* * * * * * * * *

Jupiter and Venus in 6/8: separation from the wife for a short while

Annexe 1 – Hints From Nadi

1. In Nadi we give importance to the karkatawa of a planet.
2. When a prashna chart is cast based on a basic number up to 108 or on the time of query, the Lagna shows the querent and the 9th house shows the astrologer. If the Lord of the 9th house is in debilitation or otherwise weak, the astrologer should not give prediction.
3. Planet Jupiter generally signifies males and Venus females.
4. More personally, Venus signifies the wife for a man and Mars the husband for a lady.
5. A planet in the 2H to Jupiter means that the native has younger siblings. He is the eldest when no planet occupies the 12H to Jupiter.
6. One or more planets on both sides of Jupiter mean that he has both elder and younger siblings.
7. Mars in Leo shows loss of a brother suddenly.
8. The 5th lord in the 10H means a highly placed and popular native.
9. Link between 5th and 7th Lords means either marital life is not good or children are affected. No yoga there.
10. Jupiter contacts Ketu first i.e. Jup is behind Ketu and moving forward (not vakri): the native propitiates some Goddess. If Jup is vakri, then it should be just after Ketu. There should be no planet between Jup and Ketu.
11. Using the same conditions as above, if Saturn contacts the Moon first: employment away from home.
12. For any bhava, its Kendras must have planets to fortify it.
13. From Rahu see which planet is posited next behind it. As Rahu is retrograde, the first planet behind it can be taken as entering its mouth. The native is likely to lose the relative signified by that planet first. Jupiter immediately behind Rahu means either the native is

the eldest child in one's family and if it is not so, one is likely to suffer from one's child. This child may leave the parent and live separately.

14. For Mithuna Lagna, wherever Mars is posited that bhava suffers.
15. Mercury in trine to Mars for a lady – the husband shall have another relationship.
16. A planet in exaltation with no planet flanking it loses much of its power to do well.
17. Saturn having no planet on either side or in trines to it – no fixed profession.
18. Saturn with Jupiter in the 7H: work in a big organization.
19. In a female chart, Mars behind Venus: the husband is after the wife, i.e. her husband is attached to her. He has more sexual interest.
20. In a male chart, Venus behind Mars: the wife is after the husband, i.e. she is attached to him – and she has more sexual interest.
21. Mercury and Ketu in trines: the native is likely to fall in love suddenly and that love does not materialize.
22. Moon in trine to Venus: the wife is a cheater or is cheated by others.
23. Rahu in the 2H to Venus: the wife will be obstinate and cunning. Check for other planets in the same manner. Rahu in 2H to Moon for the mother, in 2H to Sun for the father, in 2H to Mars for brother, in 2H to Mercury for friend, etc. Venus could also be the younger sister.
24. Rahu or Ketu in trines to Mars is a mangleeka dosha which indicates delay in marriage.
25. Mars in trine to Rahu in a female chart: the lady is very passionate.
26. Mars in trine to Ketu in a female chart indicates a frigid lady.
27. Sun in the 10H gives early income.

28. With Jupiter in trine to Saturn one's desires are fulfilled. Successful people.
29. Jupiter Saturn in 6/8 position is not a happy location – there can be a sudden fall as it shows misfortune and one learns to live life without much desire.
30. Jupiter closer to Saturn, i.e. in 2/12 or in 3/11 position: the native comes up early in life, one's ambitions are fulfilled. Much or at least decent contentment.
31. If Sun and Saturn are away from each other: no ambition or delay in fulfillment of one's ambitions.
32. One planet in the 10H is good and as the number of planets in the 10H increases, they show no fixed ambition.
33. Retrograde planets are powerful. They show unfinished karmas of the last life. Lots of successful people have a number of retrograde planets in their charts.
34. If Jupiter is retrograde – one has enjoyed his last birth fully. In this life such a native may become diabetic if he transgresses other's wives or takes money illegally.
35. If the dispositors of Rahu and Ketu are conjunct they act as an atom bomb: either you blow up or get blown. So Rahu/Ketu could give a big rise or a big fall.
36. The Dasha of Rahu's dispositor plays an important role in life.
37. The conjunction of any planet with Rahu or Ketu isn't good.
38. Rahu conjunct its dispositor gives potent raja yoga.
39. Rahu conjunct with Ketu's dispositor isn't desirable. Nor is Ketu conjunct with Rahu's dispositor.
40. If Rahu is in the 4H and Ketu is in the 10H, the native should not have a working wife.
41. People with Rahu in Lagna and Ketu in 7H – or vice versa, carry the karmas of their forefathers so unexpected events take place.
42. Jupiter expands the 2H from its placement.

43. Jupiter in the 4H: one's child prospers more than the native.
44. Jupiter in the 12H shows a spendthrift and taking loans.
45. Rahu in the 4H in a female chart: the husband has extracurricular activities.
46. When natal Mars is aspected by transit Moon the lady should get her monthly periods.
47. A planet in Cancer gives an elevation of this planet's karakatwas because Cancer is the sign where Jupiter is exalted.
48. With Libra Lagna, the 7th lord in Virgo is not good for the wife.
49. The 5th lord in 2H: very rich son but he is not happy.
50. No planet in Virgo means... less sickness.
51. A planet in Virgo: no love and respect from the relative signified by that planet.
52. Venus in the sign of Cancer: one of the younger sisters suffers.
53. Venus and Moon combination may destroy all yogas.
54. See which planet occupies which rashi of the D/9 chart – the relative signified by that planet dies during Saturn transit over that sign.
55. When there is a mutual exchange of two planets and a third planet conjoins any one of the exchanging planets, the relative sig- nified by the third planet suffers. If the exchange occurs between the Moon and Jupiter (Jupiter in Cancer and the Moon is in Sagittarius) with Venus conjunct the Moon, Venus' karakatwa suffers (the elder sister or the wife).
56. For a Venus in Cancer person, emotions play a major role in marital life.
57. A planet with Jupiter or Venus in a male chart gives trouble to the native or his wife as the case may be.
58. A planet with Mars or Venus in a female chart gives trouble to the husband or the native as the case may be.

59. Mars in Cancer: one purchases houses.
60. If Venus and Saturn are posited very close to each other, the native gets a wife (i.e. he gets married) and changes job (nature or place) at the same time.
61. Jupiter in trine to Ketu: spiritual inclination.
62. Ketu and the Sun in trine to Jupiter: raja yoga.
63. Jupiter in trine to Saturn and Ketu: a karma yogi. He fulfills his spiritual ambitions.
64. Jupiter in trine to Mars and Ketu: a hatha yogi – one who achieves his mission with efforts or will power.
65. Jupiter in trine to Ketu and the Moon: Bhakti yogi.
66. Saturn in trine to Ketu Mercury: Gyana yogi.
67. Saturn in trine to the Moon and Ketu: practices Sahaj yoga (patience).
68. Saturn in trine to Venus and Ketu: Sahaj yogi.
69. Rahu in Taurus means one who is very popular with the masses.
70. Rahu with the Moon: the mind is wavering.
71. Ketu with the Moon: the mind is rigid or restricted or fixed and not wavering.
72. Ketu in the 5H: whatever you desire you do not get but you are likely to get beyond your hopes.
73. When Ketu conjoins a planet, it restricts its potency.
74. When Rahu conjoins a planet it expands its activity.
75. Mercury conjunct Venus in a male chart: one has a mistress.
76. Venus in trine to Ketu: do not buy constructed property.
77. Saturn in trine to Ketu: problems in the job, but if Jupiter aspects these problems are solved.
78. Mercury in trine to Ketu: problem in educational institutions (or in education).
79. Mars in trine to Jupiter: liable for accidents.
80. Jupiter in trine to Venus: one buys a vehicle.

81. Put signatures on an agreement when transit Mercury is in trine to Jupiter or Venus.

82. Do not sign any agreement when transit Mercury is in trine to Ketu.

83. When Saturn in transit comes in trine to natal Venus: the wife falls sick.

84. When Saturn in transit comes in trine to natal Mars in a female chart: the husband falls sick.

85. Venus in trine to Rahu: the wife is arrogant and adamant and the native has to be under her thumb.

86. Venus in the 12H to Jupiter – or Venus (R) in the 2H to Jupiter in a male chart: the man does not leave his wife, he is too fond of her (Venus applies to Jupiter).

87. In chart marriage matching, see that the Sun or the Moon of the boy should fall on the Rahu or Ketu of the girl or vice versa.

88. House of fortune: Taurus // House of mind: Gemini // House of intellect: Virgo.

89. When Saturn comes over Jupiter by transit, it gives promotion and change of place.

90. Jupiter and Mars in Capricorn: one will come into possessing parental landed property.

Note: The above are collections from various NADI sources. The research students are most welcomed to try them and do further research.

Collected by:
Mr. A. V. Sundaram

Annexe 2 – Transits Of Slow Moving Grahas

RAHU & KETU

Year	Month	Day	Sign RAHU	Sign KETU
1940	Jan	1	Libra	Aries
1940	Jan	31	Virgo	Pisces
1941	Aug	13	Leo	Aquarius
1643	April	17	Cancer	Capricorn
1944	Oct	17	Gemini	Sagittarius
1946	April	8	Taurus	Scorpio
1947	Dec	20	Aries	Libra
1949	June	25	Pisces	Virgo
1950	Dec	22	Aquarius	Leo
1952	June	16	Capricorn	Cancer
1954	Feb	27	Sagittarius	Gemini
1955	Sept	4	Scorpio	Taurus
1957	Feb	24	Libra	Aries
1958	Aug	28	Virgo	Pisces
1960	May	8	Leo	Aquarius
1961	Nov	10	Cancer	Capricorn
1963	May	2	Gemini	Sagittarius
1964	Nov	9	Taurus	Scorpio
1966	July	20	Aries	Libra
1968	Jan	14	Pisces	Virgo
1969	July	10	Aquarius	Leo
1971	March	15	Capricorn	Cancer
1972	Sept	27	Sagittarius	Gemini
1974	March	20	Scorpio	Taurus
1975	Sept	18	Libra	Aries
1977	May	30	Virgo	Pisces
1978	Dec	3	Leo	Aquarius

Year	Month	Day	Sign RAHU	Sign KETU
1980	May	27	Cancer	Capricorn
1981	Nov	25	Gemini	Sagittarius
1983	Aug	14	Taurus	Scorpio
1985	Feb	5	Aries	Libra
1986	Aug	5	Pisces	Virgo
1988	Feb	2	Aquarius	Leo
1989	Oct	23	Capricorn	Cancer
1991	April	12	Sagittarius	Gemini
1992	Oct	11	Scorpio	Taurus
1994	June	9	Libra	Aries
1995	Dec	28	Virgo	Pisces
1997	June	20	Leo	Aquarius
1998	Oct	17	Cancer	Capricorn
2000	Sept	2	Gemini	Sagittarius
2002	March	2	Taurus	Scorpio
2003	Aug	29	Aries	Libra
2005	Feb	22	Pisces	Virgo
2006	Nov	13	Aquarius	Leo
2008	May	6	Capricorn	Cancer
2009	Nov	4	Sagittarius	Gemini
2011	May	4	Scorpio	Taurus
2013	Jan	15	Libra	Aries
2014	July	15	Virgo	Pisces
2016	Jan	9	Leo	Aquarius
2017	Sept	15	Cancer	Capricorn
2019	March	26	Gemini	Sagittarius
2020	Sept	22	Taurus	Scorpio
2022	March	16	Aries	Libra
2023	Dec	1	Pisces	Virgo
2025	June	2	Aquarius	Leo
2026	Nov	27	Capricorn	Cancer
2028	May	25	Sagittarius	Gemini
2030	Feb	7	Scorpio	Taurus

SATURN – SHANI

Year	Month	Day	Sign SATURN
1940	Jan	1	Aries
1941	June	19	Taurus
1941	Dec	15	Aries
1942	March	4	Taurus
1943	Aug	6	Gemini
1943	Dec	17	Taurus
1944	April	24	Gemini
1945	Sept	23	Cancer
1945	Dec	23	Gemini
1946	June	9	Cancer
1948	July	27	Leo
1950	Sept	21	Virgo
1952	Nov	26	Libra
1953	April	25	Virgo
1953	Aug	22	Libra
1955	Nov	13	Scorpio
1958	Feb	9	Sagittarius
1958	June	3	Scorpio
1958	Nov	8	Sagittarius
1961	Feb	2	Capricorn
1961	Sept	18	Sagittarius
1961	Oct	8	Capricorn
1964	Jan	28	Aquarius
1966	April	9	Pisces
1966	Nov	4	Aquarius
1966	Dec	20	Pisces
1968	June	18	Aries

Year	Month	Day	Sign SATURN
1968	Sept	29	Pisces
1969	March	8	Aries
1971	April	29	Taurus
1973	June	11	Gemini
1975	July	24	Cancer
1977	Sept	8	Leo
1979	Nov	4	Virgo
1980	March	16	Leo
1980	July	28	Virgo
1982	Oct	7	Libra
1984	Dec	22	Scorpio
1985	June	1	Libra
1985	Sept	17	Scorpio
1987	Dec	17	Sagittarius
1990	March	21	Capricorn
1990	June	21	Sagittarius
1990	Dec	15	Capricorn
1993	March	6	Aquarius
1993	Oct	16	Capricorn
1993	Nov	10	Aquarius
1995	June	3	Pisces
1995	Aug	11	Aquarius
1996	Feb	17	Pisces
1998	April	18	Aries
2000	June	7	Taurus
2002	July	24	Gemini
2003	Jan	9	Taurus
2003	April	7	Gemini

Year	Month	Day	Sign SATURN
2004	Sept	6	Cancer
2005	Jan	14	Gemini
2005	May	27	Cancer
2006	Nov	1	Leo
2007	Jan	11	Cancer
2007	July	16	Leo
2009	Sept	10	Virgo
2011	Nov	16	Libra
2012	May	16	Virgo
2012	Aug	4	Libra
2014	Nov	3	Scorpio
2017	Jan	27	Sagittarius
2017	June	22	Scorpio
2017	Oct	27	Sagittarius
2020	Jan	25	Capricorn
2022	April	30	Aquarius
2022	July	13	Capricorn
2023	Jan	18	Aquarius
2025	March	30	Pisces
2027	June	3	Aries
2027	Oct	21	Pisces
2028	Feb	24	Aries
2029	Aug	9	Taurus
2029	Oct	6	Aries
2030	April	18	Taurus

JUPITER - GURU

Year	Month	Day	Sign JUPITER
1940	Jan	1	Pisces
1940	April	17	Aries
1941	April	27	Taurus
1942	May	10	Gemini
1942	Oct	7	Cancer
1942	Dec	20	Gemini
1943	May	28	Cancer
1943	Oct	24	Leo
1944	Feb	5	Cancer
1944	June	19	Leo
1944	Nov	19	Virgo
1945	March	10	Leo
1945	July	19	Virgo
1945	Dec	20	Libra
1946	April	9	Virgo
1946	Aug	19	Libra
1947	Jan	18	Scorpio
1947	May	12	Libra
1947	Nov	18	Scorpio
1948	Feb	12	Sagittarius
1948	June	23	Scorpio
1948	Oct	8	Sagittarius
1949	March	1	Capricorn
1949	Aug	28	Sagittarius
1949	Oct	12	Capricorn
1950	March	14	Aquarius
1951	March	24	Pisces
1952	April	1	Aries
1953	April	10	Taurus

Year	Month	Day	Sign JUPITER
1953	Aug	31	Gemini
1953	Dec	1	Taurus
1954	April	20	Gemini
1954	Sept	10	Cancer
1955	Jan	29	Gemini
1955	May	4	Cancer
1955	Oct	2	Leo
1956	March	15	Cancer
1956	May	23	Leo
1956	Oct	29	Virgo
1957	April	19	Leo
1957	June	20	Virgo
1957	Nov	29	Libra
1958	May	18	Virgo
1958	July	22	Libra
1958	Dec	29	Scorpio
1959	June	23	Libra
1959	Aug	18	Scorpio
1960	Jan	23	Sagittarius
1961	Feb	11	Capricorn
1962	Feb	25	Aquarius
1963	March	8	Pisces
1964	March	15	Aries
1964	Aug	4	Taurus
1964	Oct	27	Aries
1965	March	22	Taurus
1965	Aug	6	Gemini
1966	Jan	10	Taurus
1966	March	24	Gemini
1966	Aug	22	Cancer
1967	Sept	15	Leo

Year	Month	Day	Sign JUPITER
1968	Oct	13	Virgo
1969	Nov	12	Libra
1970	Dec	12	Scorpio
1972	Jan	7	Sagittarius
1973	Jan	26	Capricorn
1974	Feb	10	Aquarius
1975	Feb	20	Pisces
1975	July	19	Aries
1975	Sept	11	Pisces
1976	Feb	26	Aries
1976	July	9	Taurus
1976	Dec	9	Aries
1977	Feb	23	Taurus
1977	July	19	Gemini
1978	Aug	6	Cancer
1979	Aug	30	Leo
1980	Sept	27	Virgo
1981	Oct	28	Libra
1982	Nov	27	Scorpio
1983	Dec	22	Sagittarius
1985	Jan	11	Capricorn
1986	Jan	26	Aquarius
1987	Feb	3	Pisces
1987	June	17	Aries
1987	Oct	26	Pisces
1988	Feb	3	Aries
1988	June	20	Taurus
1989	July	2	Gemini
1990	July	21	Cancer
1991	Aug	15	Leo
1992	Sept	12	Virgo

Year	Month	Day	Sign JUPITER
1993	Oct	13	Libra
1994	Nov	12	Scorpio
1995	Dec	8	Sagittarius
1996	Dec	27	Capricorn
1998	Jan	9	Aquarius
1998	May	26	Pisces
1998	Sept	11	Aquarius
1999	Jan	13	Pisces
1999	May	27	Aries
2000	June	3	Taurus
2001	June	17	Gemini
2002	July	6	Cancer
2003	July	31	Leo
2004	Aug	28	Virgo
2005	Sept	28	Libra
2006	Oct	28	Scorpio
2007	Nov	22	Sagittarius
2008	Dec	10	Capricorn
2009	May	2	Aquarius
2009	July	31	Capricorn
2009	Dec	20	Aquarius
2010	May	3	Pisces
2010	Nov	2	Aquarius
2010	Dec	6	Pisces
2011	May	9	Aries
2012	May	18	Taurus
2013	June	1	Gemini
2014	June	20	Cancer
2015	July	14	Leo
2016	Aug	12	Virgo
2017	Sept	13	Libra

Year	Month	Day	Sign JUPITER
2018	Oct	12	Scorpio
2019	March	30	Sagittarius
2019	April	23	Scorpio
2019	Nov	5	Sagittarius
2020	March	30	Capricorn
2020	July	1	Sagittarius
2020	Nov	21	Capricorn
2021	April	6	Aquarius
2021	Sept	15	Capricorn
2021	Nov	21	Aquarius
2022	April	14	Pisces
2023	April	22	Aries
2024	May	2	Taurus
2025	May	15	Gemini
2025	Oct	19	Cancer
2025	Nov	6	Gemini
2026	June	2	Cancer
2026	Nov	1	Leo
2027	Jan	25	Cancer
2027	June	26	Leo
2027	Nov	27	Virgo
2028	Feb	29	Leo
2028	July	25	Virgo
2028	Dec	27	Libra
2029	March	30	Virgo
2029	Aug	25	Libra
2030	Jan	25	Scorpio
2030	May	2	Libra

TAROT COURSES

A BEGINNERS ONLINE COURSE IN TAROT

Course duration : 10 weeks/ 2hrs a week
Course content :

a. Concept of tarot
b. Description of tarot cards
c. Major arcana
d. Minor arcana
e. Tarot spread
f. Timings of events through tarot
g. Meditation on tarot

Language of instruction – English
Course fees : ₹ 7000 / USD 125

AN ADVANCED ONLINE COURSE IN TAROT

Course duration : 4 weeks/ 2hrs a week
Course content :

a. Connectivity amongst tarot cards,
b. Tarot cards which denote the same event,
c. More complex spreads

Language of instruction – English
Medium of instruction – go to zoom/ online web conference
Course fees : ₹ 5000 / USD 75
Payment is accepted through PayPal
Recordings available
www.saptarishisshop.com

For more info, write to :
admin@saptarishisastrology.com

BASIC COURSE IN ASTROLOGY BEGINNERS LEVEL 1

Syllabus

1. Basic Introduction :

a) Vedang, b) Parts of Jyotish, c) Hora, d) Panchang

2. Elements :

All the 5 elements and their interaction and practical examples along with it.

3. Astronomy Related to Astrology :

a) Celestial Equator, b) Ecliptic, c) Declination, d) Day and Time

4. Planets :

a) 7 Planets + Nodes, b) Karakatwa of Planets
c) Diseases represented by Planets
d) Gems and Nature of Planets, e) Signs of Planets
f) Puranic Stories, g) Taste, h) Class, i) Gender
j) Exaltation/ Debilitation, k) Friendship/Enmity
l) Aspects

5. Houses :

a) 12 Houses, b) Types of Houses,
c) What the House represents, d) Grouping of Houses
e) Elements and Purpose of Houses, f) Types of Ascendants

6. Signs :

a) Zodiac Belt, b) 12 Rashis, c) Characteristics of Rashis
d) Gandanta

7. How to draw a chart Manually

8. Jupiter in 40th Year

Language of instruction – English
Medium of instruction – go to zoom/ online web conference
Course fees : ₹ 5750/USD 115.
Recordings available
www.saptarishisshop.com
For more info, write to :
admin@saptarishisastrology.com

BASIC COURSE IN ASTROLOGY BEGINNERS LEVEL 2

Course Content

YOGA

a) Meaning and Application, b) Different types of Yoga
c) Yoga w.r.t Sun, Moon, d) PanchaMahapurusha Yoga
e) Dhana Yoga, f) Vipreet Yoga

TRANSITS

a) What is transit, b) Favourable Positions
c) What is Vedha and Vipreet Vedha, d) How does it work

Dasha system

a) Basics of Dasha, b) How to correlate the Planets
c) Divisional Charts
d) Basics of Divisional Charts/ How to construct it
e) Basic Divisional Charts (D 9, D10, D 7, etc) explained.

Prashna

a) How to draw a Prashna Chart, b) Yogas of Prashna Chart
c) 4 types of Prashna Techniques

TWO UNKNOWN BSP TECHNIQUES

Language of instruction – English
Medium of instruction – go to zoom/ online web conference

Course fees : ₹ 5750/USD 115
Recordings available
www.saptarishisshop.com
For more info, write to
admin@saptarishisastrology.com

NADI NAKSHATRA

This course focuses on the practical application of Nakshatras to predict the timing of events using the principles of the Nadi Astrology.

Each Nakshatra, activating in certain year of life, brings a specific event to fructify in a person's life. This Nakshatra is not just the Janma Nakshatra but all the Nakshatras of all the planets in the horoscope. This technique is not known to Indians and has been in the hiding for long and it will be revealed to the Russian students of Vedic astrology. The course will be given by the founder Saptarishis Astrology & his team.

Course Level: Intermediate
Pre-requisite: Minimum 1-2 Years in Parashari with strong foundation in basics of houses and signs in Vedic astrology
Duration: 14 to 15 weeks, 2 hours a week
Language: English
Lessons: The course consists of 14 lessons of 2 hours each.
Course fees : ₹ 12000 / USD 300. Payment is accepted through PayPal.

DASHA PRAVESH COURSE

Dasha Pravesh Horoscope is the horoscope erected when a new Dasha starts.

This can be used for MahaDasha/Antar Dasha/Pratyantar Dasha also and seperate horoscopes can be created.

Sometimes a debilitated planets dasha gives brilliant results in the dasha and these all can be unearthed from the Dasha Pravesh horoscope which very few rarely use.

This is the most important tool in determining the results of the dasha and also what cannot be so easily seen in the natal horoscope can be so easily and more important minutely seen in the Dasha Pravesh horoscopes.

Our research has shown its applicability on Chara Dashas
Course Duration: 2 Weeks
Course Fees: ₹2500/USD20 + 18 % GST
Language: English
Recordings available
www.saptarishisshop.com
For more info, write to :
admin@saptarishisastrology.com

BCP AND BSP COURSE

BCP or the Brighu Chakra Paddati is the unique method of finding events in a life of a person.

The following is taught under the BCP method

a. Arudha Lagna
b. Pakka Lagna
c. Varshaphal
d. Divisional Charts
e. Cycle Lords
f. Kakshaya Lords
g. Vimshottari Dashas
h. Padma Chakra
i. Birth time rectification through BCP
j. Chandra Navamsha Nadi
k. Activation Rule Technique
l. Saturn Limping Method
m. Bhadhaka Technique
n. And Many More

BSP or Brighu Saral Paddati are the simple timing techniques which show as to when a particular planet or house would activate and effect another particular house in a specific year.

Course Duration: 12 Weeks
Course Fees: ₹12000 + 15 % Service Tax, USD 300
Language: English
Instruction Medium: go to zoom/ online web conference

Recordings are available
www.saptarishisshop.com
For more info, write to
admin@saptarishisastrology.com

Prashneeyam Course

In the Astrology field for the first time Saptarishis Astrology launched a course "PRASHNEEYAM" with unique combination of Prashna Marga (An epic book of "Prashna shastra") and "Krishneeyam" (A book by Alok Jagawat based on the Kerala Prashna shastra).

By this course an astrologer can educate themselves that how to do accurate prediction through Horrary Astrology (Prashna Shastra). This course is available in both English and Hindi versions.

The contents of the course.

- Introduction Horary Astrology
- Qualities of astrologer and Querist
- Birth Horoscope and Prashna Horoscope
- General principles of Horary Astrology
- ArudhaPrashna
- Introduction to AshtamangalaPrashna
- Introduction to Deva Prashna
- Fructification of Karma
- Medical Astrology in Horary Astrology
- VivahPrashna - Matrimony and Horary Astrology
- Santana Prashna - Progeny and Horary Astrology
- Profession and Business in Horary Astrology
- Chora Prashna -Theft and recovery of missing articles
- BaadhaPrashna - Invisible Obstructions
- Parihara – Remedies in Horary Astrology

Course Speakers:

1. Sunil John
2. Vinayak Bhatt
3. Neeraj Verma

Duration: 16 Weeks (Two hours/Week) + Q&A Session

Website: www.saptarishisshop.com | www.saptarishisastrology.com

Vedic Astrology

Beginner's Course

Beginner's course in Vedic Astrology is the entry level course of Vedic Astrology who doesn't know anything about the Astrology. The course will cover the complete Vedic Astrology aspects from the scratch. And this course is packed with world's best speakers/Teachers who are having very good experience in the astrology.

The contents of the course

1. Introduction Of Astrology
2. Jyotish Limbs : Ganita Skandba; Sambita Skandha; Hora Skandha; Gola; Ganita; Jataka; Prasbna; Mnhurta; Nimitta
3. The Grahas (PLANETS)
4. Planetary Aspcts& Associations
5. Strength
6. Characteristics
7. The Rashis
8. The Bhavas
9. The panchanga
10. The Nakshatras
11. Interpretation of the Horoscope
12. Placement of Lords of Houses
13. Punch Maha Purush Yogas
14. Planetary Yogas
15. Dasha &Gochar(Transit)
16. Navamsa and Hidden Techniques of Using It
17. Ashtakvarga
18. Special lacture on Kuja dosha
19. Laghu jataka
20. Laghu Parashari

Course Speakers:

1. Sunil John
2. Upendra Badhoriya
3. Vinayak Bhat
4. Neeraj Verma
5. Vidhaan Pandey

Duration: 16 Weeks (2 hours/Week)

Website: www.saptarishisshop.com | www.saptarishisastrology.com

Advance Vedic Vastu

Contents of the Course

1. 32 possible entrances in a building.
2. Effect of each entry on the residents of the building
3. How to find the entry is it good or bad for you?
4. How to correct the wrong entry
5. What are different Vritis in Vastu and how to identify them in a floor plan?
6. 45 devtas of Vastu Purush Mandal
7. Properties of each Vastudevta and how an imbalance in them effect us?
8. How to find the location of each devta in the building? VastuPadVinyas
9. How to do remedy of Vastu defect using different techniques?

Course Speakers:
Hanish Bagga

Easy Predictive Astrology

Learn step by step Interpretation of Horoscope

Contents of the Course

1. Timings of events through Vimshottari Dasha
2. Timings of Events through Bhrigu Chakra Paddhati
3. Timings of Events through Yogini Dasha.
4. Secrets of Using Karaka Planets in Timing of events
5. Secrets of Parashari and Bhrigu jyotish.

Language: English and Hindi

Course Speakers:
Vinayak Bhatt

Saptarishis Publications

Catalogue 2021

Krishneeyam

By Alok Jagawat

Rs. 425

Dasamsa in Astrology

By Late Shri R. K. Das

Rs. 425

Timing of Marriage with Tested Techniques

Dr. Nemani Venkata Raghunath Rao

Rs. 300/-

Predicting through Nakshatras Part - I

Saptarishis Astrology

Rs. 350/-

One Minute Prashna

R.K. Das

Rs. 350/-

Easy Prashna Secrets

Prabodh Purohit

Rs. 499/-

Astrology of Education

V. P. Goel

Rs. 300/-

Akshaya Lagna Paddhati

By Deepak SP

Rs. 399

Website: www.saptarishisshop.com | www.saptarishisastrology.com

Predict Everything using A Rare and Unknown Dasa

Ashutosh Bhardwaj

Rs. 350/-

Predicting through Nakshatras Part - 2

Sunil John
Vidhan Pandya

Rs. 499/-

Pulippani Jothidham

Nakkirar Natarajan

Rs. 399/-

A New Method on Birth Time Rectification

Shri R.K.Das

Rs. 225/-

Sadhu Paddhati

R. K. Das

Rs. 350/-

A New Method Timing Events using Nadi Nakshatras

Saptarishi Astrology

Rs. 350/-

Astrology & Vastu Remedies

Renu Sharma
Vishal Sharma

Rs. 350/-

Tarot

Anuradha Sharda

Rs. 350/-

Website: www.saptarishisshop.com | www.saptarishisastrology.com

Bhrighu Saral Paddathi

English

Sunil John

Rs. 600/-

Bhrighu Saral Paddathi

Hindi Part - I

Rs. 300/-

Timing of Events Using Eclipses

Prabodh Purohit

Rs. 351/-

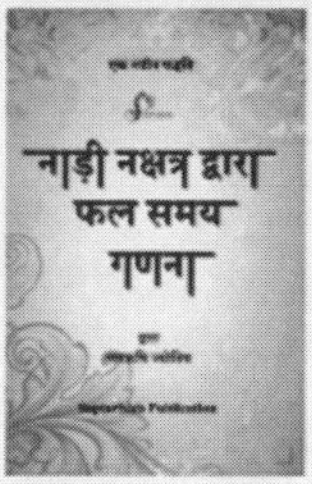

Nadi Nakshatra

Hindi

Saptarishis Astrology

Rs. 351/-

Insights in Nadi

Saptarishis Astrology

Rs. 351/-

New Marvels of Nadi Astrology

Jitendra Trivedi

Rs. 300/-

Nadi Antarvichar

Rs. 150/-

Parul Sutram

R.K.Das

Rs. 550/-

New Research in Timing of Events Using Chara & Yogini Dasha

V.P. Goel

Rs. 300/-

27 Nakshatras 27 Days

English / Hindi

Anuradha Sharda

Rs. 99/- (each)

Simple Remedies For Planetary Afflictions in Kashi and other Places

Lalitha V

Rs. 125/-

Laghu Parashari & Madhya Parashari

Chandrashekhar Sharma

Rs. 250/-

Chakravyuh planetary Influences

Satish K. Navathe

Rs. 700/-

Pratical Nadi Astrology

Satyamma Bhardwaj

Rs. 300/-

Astrology The Divine Order of the Universe

Joni Patry

Rs. 300/-

How to Make Money Using Astrology

Joni Patry

Rs. 300/-

Website: www.saptarishisshop.com | www.saptarishisastrology.com

Saptarishis Astrology

World's Premier Astrology
Free Digital Magazine
As Read in 120 Countries

Invites Rare Astrology Articles in All Languages

Saptatrishis Astrology is an annual multi-lingual Astrological E-Magazine. We are a free global platform to astrologers worldwide: Vedic astrologers as well as Western astrologers. In short span to span Saptarishis Astrology has become the most premiere astrology magazine in the world due to the hard work of the global volunteer astrologers.

- Saptarishis Astrology is the first magazine to allow the authors to retain the copyright of their articles. This magazine is available at www.saptarishisastrology.com contains astrology (Jyotish) articles of various categories like Indian Astrology, Western Astrology, Bhrigu Saral Paddhati, Bhrigu Chakra Paddhati, Nadi Astrology etc.
- Free download of manuscripts on Parasara, Jaimini and Nadi Astrology.
- Free database of charts on various categories of horoscopes.
- Send your articles to admin@saptarishisastrology.com

Saptarishis Astrology YouTube Channel

Where The Greatest Of Astrologers Meet & Share Their Knowledge

To Subscribe copy paste this link on your browser:

https://www.youtube.com/user/AstrologySaptarishis

Please don't forget to hit the subscribe button.

Saptarishis Astrology's YouTube channel brings out unique and rare astrological knowledge to its subscriber and viewers. Video interviews and webinars of top astrologers are released for benefit of one and all. Hundreds of master techniques are demonstrated on common, as well as celebrity horoscopes, presented and taught by so many great masters of astrology like Shri. K.N.Rao, Shri A.V. Sundaram, Smt. Gayatri Devi Vasudev, Shri Naleen Desai, Justice Shri S.N.Kapoor, Dr. Shri Suresh Chandra Mishra, Shri Prabodh Purohit, Shri. Virji Gala, Shri Sunil Ghaisas, Shri V.P. Goel, Dr. Shri Vasant Lad, Smt. Mrs. Kundan Desai, Ryan Kurczak, James Braha, Shri Sunil Pandey, Shri Nitin Kashyap, Ksanati Nakshatra, Shri Visti Larsen, Shri Dennis Harness and many more through the distinct and diverse interview series.

Like Saptarishis Astrology online magazine, Saptarishis' YouTube channel has gained attention of people from all over the world. Every week, Saptarishis's YouTube channel brings out 2-3 new videos which are not to be missed by true students of astrology. Saptarishis Astrology thanks its subscribers and viewers for their support and encouragement and encourage serious students of astrology to Subscribe our channel.

For Online Shopping:
www.saptarishisshop.com

Download the Saptarishis Astrology App Now

For Latest Updates

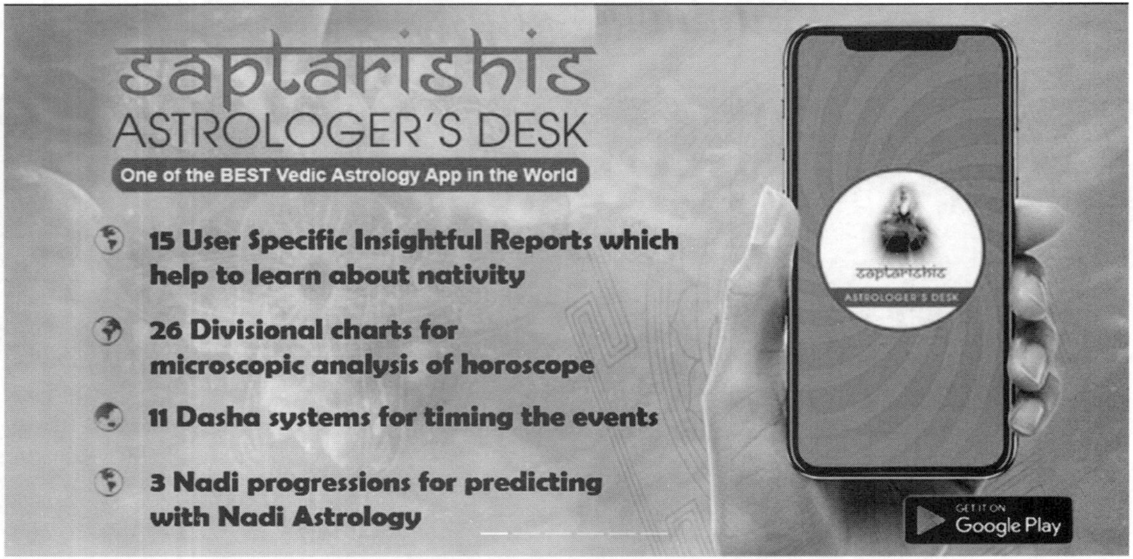

https://saptarishis.net/